examining the psychological components

THE ENCYCLOPEDIA OF PSYCHOLOGICAL DISORDERS

Senior Consulting Editor Carol C. Nadelson, M.D.
Consulting Editor Claire E. Reinburg

CHILD
ABUSE
and
NEGLECT
examining the psychological components

Elizabeth Russell Connelly

CHELSEA HOUSE PUBLISHERS
Philadelphia

The ENCYCLOPEDIA OF PSYCHOLOGICAL DISORDERS provides up-to-date information on the history of, causes and effects of, and treatment and therapies for problems affecting the human mind. The titles in this series are not intended to take the place of the professional advice of a psychiatrist or mental health care professional.

Chelsea House Publishers
Editor in Chief: Stephen Reginald
Managing Editor: James D. Gallagher
Production Manager: Pamela Loos
Art Director: Sara Davis
Director of Photography: Judy L. Hasday
Senior Production Editor: Lee Anne Gelletly

Staff for CHILD ABUSE AND NEGLECT
Picture Researcher: Patricia Burns
Associate Art Director: Takeshi Takahashi
Cover Designer: Brian Wible

The Chelsea House World Wide Web site address is
http://www.chelseahouse.com

First Printing

9 8 7 6 5 4 3 2

Library of Congress Cataloging-in-Publication Data

Connelly, Elizabeth Russell.
Child abuse and neglect / Elizabeth Russell Connelly.
  p.cm. —(Encyclopedia of psychological disorders)
Includes bibliographical references and index.
Summary: Discusses the nature, history, and causes of child abuse and neglect
and the impact of this problem on society.
ISBN 0-7910-4955-8 (hc)
1. Child abuse—United States—Juvenile literature. 2. Abused children—United States—
Juvenile literature. [1. Child abuse.] I. Title. II. Series: Connelly, Elizabeth Russell.
Encyclopedia of Psychological Disorders.
HV6626.52.C65 1999
362.76'0973—dc21

                                                          98–53702
                                                            CIP
                                                            AC

CONTENTS

PSYCHOLOGICAL DISORDERS AND THEIR EFFECT

CAROL C. NADELSON, M.D.
PRESIDENT AND CHIEF EXECUTIVE OFFICER,
The American Psychiatric Press

There are a wide range of problems that are considered psychological disorders, including mental and emotional disorders, problems related to alcohol and drug abuse, and some diseases that cause both emotional and physical symptoms. Psychological disorders often begin in early childhood, but during adolescence we see a sharp increase in the number of people affected by these disorders. It has been estimated that about 20 percent of the U.S. population will have some form of mental disorder sometime during their lifetime. Some psychological disorders appear following severe stress or trauma. Others appear to occur more often in some families and may have a genetic or inherited component. Still other disorders do not seem to be connected to any cause we can yet identify. There has been a great deal of attention paid to learning about the causes and treatments of these disorders, and exciting new research has taught us a great deal in the past few decades.

The fact that many new and successful treatments are available makes it especially important that we reject old prejudices and outmoded ideas that consider mental disorders to be untreatable. If psychological problems are identified early, it is possible to prevent serious consequences. We should not keep these problems hidden or feel shame that we or a member of our family has a mental disorder. Some people believe that something they said or did caused a mental disorder. Some people think that these disorders are "only in your head" so that you could "snap out of it" if you made the effort. This type of thinking implies that a treatment is a matter of willpower or motivation. It is a terrible burden for someone who is suffering to be blamed for his or her misery, and often people with psychological disorders are not treated compassionately. We hope that the information in this book will teach you about various mental illnesses.

The problems covered in the volumes of the ENCYCLOPEDIA OF PSYCHOLOGICAL DISORDERS were selected because they are of particular importance to young adults, because they affect them directly, or because they affect family and friends. There are individual volumes on reading disorders, attention deficit and disruptive behavior disorders, and dementia—all of these are related to our abilities to learn and integrate information from the world around us. There are books on drug abuse that provide useful information about the effects of these drugs and treatments that are available for those individuals who have drug problems. Some of the books concentrate on one of the most common mental disorders, depression. Others deal with eating disorders, which are dangerous illnesses that affect a large number of young adults, especially women.

Most of the public attention paid to these disorders arises from a particular incident involving a celebrity that awakens us to our own vulnerability to psychological problems. These incidents of celebrities or public figures revealing their own psychological problems can also enable us to think about what we can do to prevent and treat these types of problems.

This three-year-old girl is one of the many tragic victims of child abuse; in October 1998 she was beaten to death by her mother and two neighbors. Each year in the United States, approximately 2,000 children die as a result of abuse.

CHILD ABUSE AND NEGLECT: AN OVERVIEW

Child abuse has been a fact of life throughout history; however, recognition of abuse as a pervasive, traumatizing problem has come slowly. This has been due in large part to society's tendency to deny or ignore its existence. But 19th-century activists demanded a closer look at the tragedy of child abuse. Our understanding of how children are abused has gradually evolved and changed. Today we generally refer to four categories of child maltreatment—neglect, emotional and mental abuse, physical abuse, and sexual abuse.

Neglect involves failure to provide appropriate food, shelter, clothing, education, supervision, or health care. Emotional abuse usually refers to a parent's belittling or shaming the child, as well as parental failure to support or respond emotionally to the child. Physical abuse encompasses both major and minor injuries to the body. Sexual abuse may include sexual intercourse, molestation, or other sexual maltreatment, often by a family member or authority figure. The boundaries are blurred in many cases of abuse and they often coexist. Children who suffer physical maltreatment are also likely to suffer neglect and emotional abuse; those enduring sexual abuse often fall victim to physical battering and mental and emotional manipulation.

The purpose of this volume is to give readers outside the field of psychology a better understanding of child abuse. A look at recent statistics shows why this understanding is necessary:

- The findings from a 1996 study indicate that, out of the 22.3 million adolescents in the United States today, 1.8 million have been victims of serious sexual assault, 3.9 million have been victims of serious physical assault, and almost 9 million adolescents have witnessed serious violence.

- In *The Commonwealth Fund Survey of the Health of*

Adolescent Girls (1997), one in five high school girls reported that she had been physically or sexually abused. The majority of the abuse occurred at home (53 percent) and more than once (65 percent). Nearly a third had not told anyone about the abuse.

- According to the *Third National Incidence Study of Child Abuse and Neglect* (1996), girls are sexually abused three times more often than boys. However, boys are more likely to die or be seriously injured from physical abuse.

- The risk of being sexually abused does not vary among races; and abuse of all types occurs in families of all income levels, although children from lower income groups are more frequently victims.

Clearly, too many of our society's children are victims of abuse, and reports of child maltreatment are on the rise. In the past many incidents went unreported, as most people considered child abuse a problem best handled privately by the family. But over the past few decades, greater public awareness has led to a greater number of concerned family members, friends, teachers, and neighbors reporting suspected abuse to authorities. According to a 1996 survey by the National Committee to Prevent Child Abuse, a case of child abuse was reported every 10 seconds, for a total of more than 3.1 million reports and nearly 1 million confirmed victims. Of the substantiated cases, 60 percent suffered neglect; 23 percent physical abuse; 9 percent sexual abuse; 4 percent emotional maltreatment; and 5 percent other forms of abuse.

Many children know almost nothing but abuse in their short lives. In one year alone some 2,000 American children—approximately five each day—die from physical abuse or neglect. According to the U.S. Advisory Board on Child Abuse and Neglect, in the first five years of the 1990s, 10,000 American children died at the hands of their parents or caretakers. This type of maltreatment has become a leading cause of death for young children, outstripping deaths caused by car wrecks, fires, and drowning.

The numbers speak volumes about violence in our society. But who is committing such heinous acts? Traditionally, parents—and adult men in particular—have been considered the main culprits. While this still appears to be true, recognition of other assailants is on the rise.

Adolescents, usually males, and often siblings or schoolmates, are being identified more and more with the abuse of younger children. While some assaults are homosexual, many perpetrators don't seem to care whether they abuse boys or girls. What matters to them is that the victims are powerless children. Though still very rare, cases of male adolescents (and children) who are sexually abused by adult women are more commonly acknowledged and treated than ever before.

In this volume of the ENCYCLOPEDIA OF PSYCHOLOGICAL DISORDERS, we attempt to answer the most fundamental questions about child maltreatment. Chapter 1 provides an overview, highlighting the types of abuse and discussing how they differ and sometimes overlap. Chapter 2 traces the history of child abuse, mainly from a legislative point of view, in an attempt to provide readers with some perspective on the evolution of this crime in our society.

Many of us may see the signs, perhaps the scars, of abuse in children at school or maybe even among siblings and relatives, but we don't know how the victims actually feel. On the other hand, some readers may have picked up this book because they themselves are the victims of abuse. For those concerns, chapter 3 provides examples and descriptions of how victims are affected, including several case studies, so that readers can gain insight by reading about the real-life struggles faced by other adolescents like themselves. In chapter 4 we take a look at who commits such tragic acts against children and common reasons why abuse begins. Chapter 5 examines sexual abuse and abusers.

Chapter 6 explores the ways child abuse affects society as a whole, in both social and financial terms. Finally, in chapter 7, we highlight the various means of treating the emotional and psychological damage and behavioral problems associated with child abuse, closing with a discussion of how to prevent abuse in the first place.

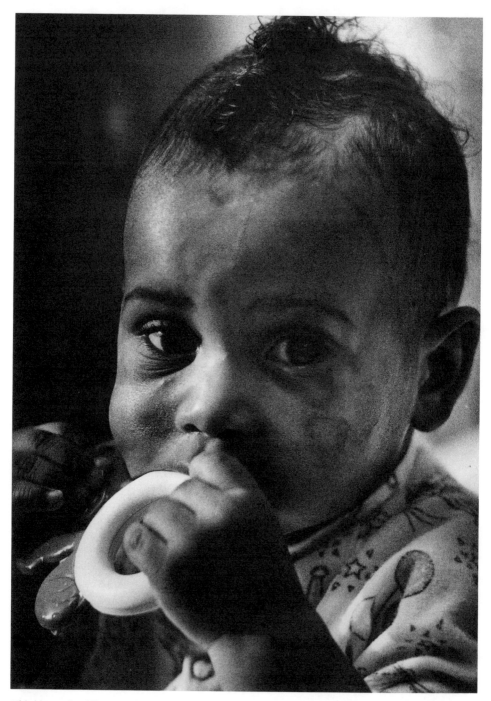

This battered toddler was abandoned by his mother outside a Michigan grocery store. Child abuse and neglect are two very serious problems today: each year, over one million children are victims of abuse or neglect.

1

WHAT IS CHILD ABUSE?

A buse can be hard to define. Whether a particular action constitutes abuse depends on both the circumstances and the attitudes of the society in which that action occurs. Until the 1980s, physical punishment and beatings were widely accepted methods of discipline, even for small children, in the United States and other countries. Now many parents are forgoing physical punishment. In fact, a 1995 survey of families in the United States found that the number of parents who spank or hit their children has dropped by 17 percent (from 64 percent to 47 percent) from 1988. Attitudes toward hitting or physically abusing children are also changing in other nations. For example, in Sweden parents are forbidden by law to spank or slap a child for any reason.

Despite this trend toward nonphysical punishment, child abuse continues to occur much too frequently. Investigations by child protective services agencies in 49 U.S. states determined that in 1995 more than 1 million children were victims of child abuse and neglect. Based on reports received and investigated by child protective services agencies in 1995, about 15 of every 1,000 children younger than 18 were found to be victims of abuse or neglect.

Ominously, these numbers refer only to those abuse cases that are reported. Several studies suggest that even more children suffer from abuse or neglect than official statistics reflect. The *Third National Incidence Study of Child Abuse and Neglect*, a federal study involving 5,600 community professionals who come into contact with children, estimated that as many as 42 children per 1,000 may have been victims of abuse or neglect in 1993. A 1995 telephone survey of parents conducted by the Gallup Poll estimated that as many as 49 children per 1,000 endure physical abuse, and 19 per 1,000 suffer sexual abuse. Emotional abuse is much more difficult to quantify, but it is usually a by-product of these other forms of abuse.

The term *child abuse* was originally conceived to describe physical battering of children or adolescents. That phrase now encompasses many forms of abuse—physical, sexual, and emotional—as well as parental neglect. Although the legal definitions of "child abuse" and "neglect" may vary from state to state, abuse usually occurs when a parent purposefully harms a child. Thus physical actions such as hitting or kicking a child would likely constitute abuse, although in most cases parents would not be considered abusive if they discipline their child with a slap or a spanking that does not cause physical injury. Neglect arises from a parent's passive indifference to a child's well-being. Leaving a helpless child alone or failing to feed him or her for a long period of time would qualify as neglect. The popular movie *Home Alone* and its sequels are intended to be humorous, but many observers were horrified by the apparent negligence and uncaring behavior of the parents in the film, who didn't notice their child's absence for hours. This sort of behavior in real life would be considered neglect.

In order to better understand the distinction between the four major types of child maltreatment—physical abuse, sexual abuse, child neglect, and emotional abuse—refer to the following sections, which provide an overview of each.

PHYSICAL ABUSE

In general, most laws define *physical abuse* as the infliction of injury on a person under 18 by a parent or legally responsible caretaker. A parent or guardian who allows such injury to take place is also considered abusive. Such physical injury might result from punching, beating, kicking, biting, burning, shaking, or otherwise harming a child. In many cases the parent or caretaker may not have intended to hurt the child, but injury can still occur from excessive discipline or physical punishment.

A study of 665 children (ages 9 to 17) and their parents or guardians provides some examples of how a child might be abused. In interviews examiners used the following categories to define physical abuse. A child has been abused if he or she has been:

- Hit very hard on more than five occasions
- Beaten, kicked, badly bruised, severely injured, or has had bones broken
- Locked in a room for five hours or more, or told that he or she would not have food for a whole day or longer
- The victim of some other harsh physical punishment

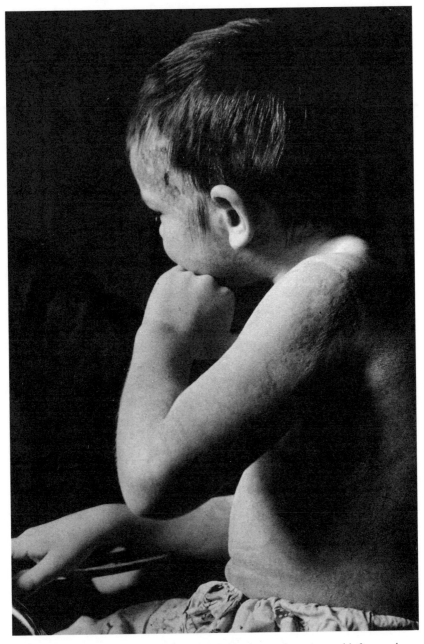

This child has been severely beaten, and shows bruises and scarring on his face and back. The term "child abuse" was originally used to describe physical battering of children or adolescents. This term is now used to cover physical, sexual, and emotional abuse, as well as parental neglect.

Using these categories, this study, which covered children living in New York State and Puerto Rico, found that 172 of the 665 youths surveyed (26 percent) had been physically abused. When the children were asked specifically how they had been abused, they responded as follows: 67 percent said that they had been hit very hard; 15 percent had been beaten or kicked; nearly 11 percent had been locked in a room for five hours or more or told that they would not have food for a whole day or longer; and 7 percent had bones broken or had been severely injured.

SEXUAL ABUSE

Child *sexual abuse* is any sexual behavior directed toward a child or adolescent under 18 by a person who has power over that youth. Such behavior always involves a betrayal of the child's trust. Sexual abuse that involves physical contact could entail fondling the child's genitals, getting the child to fondle the offender's genitals, rubbing the offender's genitals on the child, engaging in oral sex, or making anal or vaginal penetration. There are also nonphysical forms of sexual abuse, including exhibitionism (when a person shows his or her genitals to a child); the showing of *pornography* (sexually explicit pictures or videotapes) to a child, or the involvement of a child in the creation of pornographic materials; and sexual suggestiveness. Parents or caretakers who allow another person to perform any of the abusive actions listed above with their young child are also regarded as sexually abusive.

Sexual abusers aren't necessarily strangers. They are often people in positions of power or trust: parents or stepparents, siblings or other relatives, teachers, baby-sitters, neighbors, peers, clergymen, or doctors. In fact, boys and girls are most often abused by adults or older children whom they know and who can control them, or an authority figure whom they trust or love. In eight out of ten reported cases, the victim knows his or her abuser. In many cases the child is convinced to engage in sex or other abusive actions by means of persuasion, bribes, or threats. Many experts believe that sexual abuse is the most underreported form of child maltreatment because of the silence and secrecy that so often characterize such experiences.

CHILD NEGLECT

Neglect occurs when parents or caretakers do not provide for a child's basic needs—physically, educationally, or emotionally.

Physical neglect may involve inadequate supervision or *abandonment*

MYTHS AND FACTS
ABOUT SEXUAL ABUSE

Myth: Children lie about sexual abuse.

Fact: Studies have shown that in more than 94 percent of cases, children's reports of sexual abuse have been confirmed by independent investigation. The truth is, children are often reluctant to discuss what has happened to them.

Myth: Strangers present a greater danger of abuse.

Fact: Children are more likely to be abused by someone they know. Studies show that 75 to 80 percent of abuse cases involve someone known to the victim.

Myth: The abuser is a "dirty old man."

Fact: Research suggests that many perpetrators are young heterosexual males who come from all types of socioeconomic backgrounds. Most appear to be no different from other men in the community.

Myth: Children are seductive and provoke abuse.

Fact: This inaccurate belief takes responsibility for abuse away from the adult and places it on the child. Adults are more mature and knowledgeable than children; they always have a choice in how they will react to a child's behavior. The perpetrator is always responsible for the abuse.

Myth: Reporting the abuse causes trauma in the child's life.

Fact: Concerns about outside intervention in children's lives are valid, and so are concerns about the traumatic effects of becoming involved in the legal system. However, this cannot be used as an excuse for adults not to act and protect the child from further abuse. Continued abuse will cause more traumatic effects during the child's life than will stopping the abuse and taking steps to punish the perpetrator.

Myth: Sexual abuse is harmless to children.

Fact: Sexually abused children often have problems with aggressive behavior, depression, and social withdrawal, as well as emotional damage. Adult survivors of child abuse often experience depression, low self-esteem, and difficulty in forming and maintaining relationships.

—Source: U.S. Department of Health and Human Services

A Wisconsin couple was charged with child abuse in November 1997 for keeping their seven-year-old daughter in this dog cage in their basement as punishment. Emotional abuse, which includes bizarre forms of punishment like this case, may cause children to develop serious psychological problems as they grow older.

(desertion) of the child. The abusive parent may not take a sick or injured child to a doctor or hospital, or the parent may force a child out of the home or refuse to allow a runaway to return home.

Forms of educational neglect include allowing a child to be chronically truant, failing to enroll a child of mandatory school age in school, and ignoring or denying a child special educational needs such as additional classes to help him or her overcome a learning disorder.

Repeatedly depriving a child of affection qualifies as emotional neglect. Other examples of this type of neglect are refusing or failing to provide necessary psychological care, abusing a spouse in the child's presence, or permitting the child to use drugs or alcohol in the home.

EMOTIONAL ABUSE

Emotional abuse—also called "psychological abuse," "verbal abuse," or "mental injury"—involves actions (or nonactions) by parents or other caregivers that may cause their child to develop serious behavioral, emotional, or mental disorders. For example, the parents/caregivers may use extreme or bizarre forms of punishment, such as confinement of a child in a dark closet or hanging a young child from a wall hook, that torture the child emotionally. Less severe acts, such as habitually blaming the child for the parent's actions or belittling him or her, are often difficult to prove; therefore, the abuse may go undetected by others, leaving the child to suffer in silence.

SIMILARITIES AND DIFFERENCES BETWEEN FORMS OF ABUSE

Forms of child maltreatment often occur in combination. In fact, many studies consider physical abuse and neglect together, and emotional abuse is almost always present when other forms are identified.

Physical and sexual abuse are similar to the extent that they involve the intentional misuse or exploitation of a child by a parent or caretaker in an unhealthy family environment. Both types of abuse can be prosecuted—usually in either family court or juvenile court, although sexual abuse and the most severe cases of physical abuse may be prosecuted in a criminal court. In general, physicians and teachers (or other professionals involved in a child's care) who suspect the occurrence of either physical or sexual abuse are required to report it to designated authorities that deal with child abuse.

The victims of sexual and physical abuse differ in several ways. Most cases of sexual abuse involve a male authority figure and a young female, while physical abuse is committed almost equally by male and female adults against equal numbers of boys and girls. Sexual victimization is more likely to go undiscovered, because it's less likely to result in a visible physical injury, and children and family members are less apt to disclose sexual abuse, given the greater degree of guilt and the stigma associated with it.

PORTRAIT OF ABUSERS AND THEIR VICTIMS

In November 1998 the U.S. Department of Health and Human Services issued a national study of child abuse, *Child Maltreatment 1996: Reports from the States to the National Child Abuse and Neglect Data System*. The report found that child protective services agencies

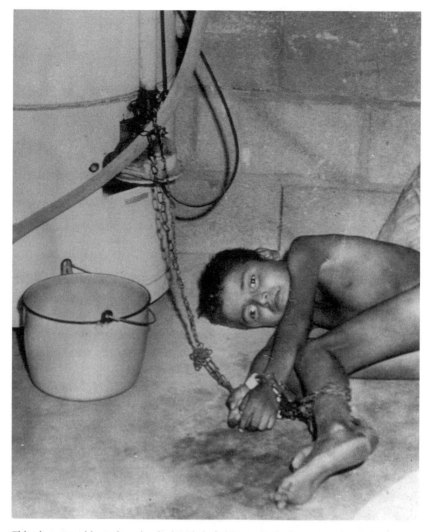

This nine-year-old was found naked and chained to a washing machine in the basement of his Texas home. "Whenever mother leaves the house she ties me up," he told police. Types of abuse often overlap: in addition to being beaten and neglected, this child suffered the emotional abuse of being confined alone in the basement.

investigated more than two million reports of abuse or maltreatment, involving more than three million children. These investigations showed that about a million children were victims of abuse in 1996. Almost two-thirds of the substantiated reports came from professional sources—teachers, law enforcement officials, doctors and nurses, or social service workers. The report noted that the number of children who suffered abuse had increased approximately 18 percent since 1990.

The government's statistics also present a profile of the victims of child abuse. More than half (52 percent) of the victims suffered neglect, and 24 percent suffered physical abuse. About 12 percent of the victims were sexually abused. Nine percent suffered from medical neglect or emotional maltreatment. Most of the victims of neglect or medical neglect were younger than eight years old, while the greater proportion of victims of physical, sexual, and emotional abuse were older than eight.

The largest percentage of abused children were white (53 percent), followed by African Americans (27 percent), and Hispanics (11 percent). Abused children of Native Americans or natives of Alaska made up 2 percent of the victim pool, and Asian children comprised about 1 percent. "The percentages of African American and American Indian/Alaska Native victims were disproportionately high, almost twice their representation in the national child population," the government report states.

In the United States there were 1,077 child abuse-related fatalities in 1996. Children younger than age four accounted for 76 percent of these deaths.

Regarding abusers, the government report found that 77 percent were parents and an additional 11 percent were related to the victim. More than 80 percent of the perpetrators were under age 40, and almost two-thirds were females. The study found that about three-quarters of neglect and medical neglect cases were associated with female abusers, while nearly 75 percent of sexual abuse cases involved men.

Abuse of children has been occurring for many years, as this 1881 drawing, titled The Brute and the Lamb, *illustrates. However, it was not until recent decades that child abuse and neglect have been recognized as serious social problems.*

2

HISTORY OF CHILD ABUSE

Although child abuse has existed throughout history, it took several centuries and much controversy before abuse became a concern of the general public. A fundamental reason for this lies in the definition of abuse, which continues to evolve over time and across cultures. For instance, before child labor laws went into effect in the United States during the 19th century's Industrial Revolution, it was common for very young children to work 14-hour days in factories. Although today this practice would be considered abusive, at the time allowing young children to help support the family through factory work was acceptable.

The earliest clinical documentation of child abuse occurred in 1860, when French forensic physician Ambroise Tardieu published an exposé on battered children. He later published works on rape and childhood sexual abuse as well. At the time, he was denounced by his contemporaries for treating what was then considered "discipline," a private family matter, as child abuse. A decade later in England, Josephine Butler campaigned against child prostitution, comparing the traffic in children to the slave trade. She was harassed by London police and assaulted by owners of brothels. Such reactions to attempts at bringing child abuse to the public consciousness later caused Richard K. Summit, a professor of psychiatry at UCLA, to note, "Since 1860, child abuse has been discovered and then discredited every 35 years by the most visionary clinicians of the day, each faced with the alternative of denouncing the discovery or succumbing to scorn and disgrace."

Studies conducted in the first half of this century confirm the findings of 19th-century researchers and activists: Child abuse, and sexual abuse in particular, is an age-old problem. A 1938 study of 752 women found that 38 percent of the group had been sexually abused before age 15. Fifteen years later, in 1953, 24 percent of the 4,441 women interviewed for another study acknowledged that they had been sexually abused during childhood.

Child labor was a sordid, but recognized, fact of American life until the late 1930s. These scenes show a young girl working in a textile mill and adolescent boys employed to separate shale and slate from coal at a mine.

Although early advocates of children's rights struggled to protect children by raising awareness of the problems of abuse and neglect, in the late 19th century the father of psychoanalysis, Sigmund Freud, brought the discussion of child abuse to the forefront. Freud was the first doctor to become widely recognized for his research and writings on child abuse; in his book *The Aetiology of Hysteria,* published in 1896, he identified child sexual abuse as the cause of much mental and emotional illness in adulthood. Unfortunately, after significant ridicule and criticism from his colleagues, Freud recanted his conclusions, maintaining instead that his patients' stories were merely fantasies they must have fabricated.

It was not until 1910 that the issue of sexual abuse began to be taken somewhat seriously in the United States. That year Congress passed the Mann Act (also known as the White Slave Traffic Act), which prohibited transportation of women and children across state lines for "immoral purposes"—namely, sexual exploitation. However, claims of sexual abuse by children were still generally considered fantasies and were usually met with denial by family members or authorities. Even when a claim of sexual assault was believed, generally either the child was blamed for attracting such attention or the incident was downplayed by the rest of the family. This attitude of skepticism and suspicion continued for several decades.

THE PROBLEM OF CHILD LABOR

Efforts to restrict other forms of abuse, such as overworking children, began in the 19th century. In 1836, Massachusetts passed a law requiring that working children receive some schooling. In 1842, Massachussets and Connecticut limited the work of children in textile factories to 10 hours a day, and in 1848, Pennsylvania made it illegal for children under 12 to work in factories. However, despite these early reforms there were still hundreds of thousands of children working in the United States. The 1870 census reported 750,000 workers under 15, and this did not include the many children who helped out with family farms, stores, or other businesses. Over the next 40 years, the number of child workers, and their percentage of the population of children in the United States, increased. Hugh G. Cleland, of the State University of New York at Stony Brook, described the situation 100 years ago:

By 1900 about half of the states placed some sorts of restrictions on child labor, but only about 10 made a serious effort to enforce such laws as there were. The South was finally industrializing . . . .[and] the number of child laborers in the South tripled between 1890 and 1900.

Elsewhere in the country, the glass industry employed young boys for 12-hour shifts in front of fiery furnaces. The domestic system lingered on in the garment industry where whole families labored for subcontractors in tenement sweatshops. In the coalfields, boys . . . . sat hunched over chutes as coal poured beneath them, picked out the stone and slate, and breathed coal dust for 10 hours at a stretch. The tobacco industry employed thousands of children under 10 to make cigars and cigarettes. In silk spinning, artificial flower making, oyster shucking, berry picking, canning, and shrimp packing, the story was the same.

The National Child Labor Committee (NCLC) was established in 1904 by social workers determined to end this abuse. The NCLC began lobbying for a national law regulating child labor. In 1912, Congress established a Children's Bureau, and in 1916 it passed the Owen-Keating Act. This law forbade interstate commerce in goods on which children under age 14 had worked or on which 14- to 16-year-olds had worked more than eight hours per day. However, two years later the Supreme Court ruled in the case of *Hammer v. Dagenhart* that Owen-Keating was an unconstitutional encroachment on states' rights. A similar law was introduced in 1919, and again overturned in 1922. Child labor regulations were incorporated into part of Franklin D. Roosevelt's New Deal program in 1933, but lasting child labor reforms would not occur until later in that decade.

In 1938, the Fair Labor Standards Act was passed by Congress. This legislation and its amendments constitute the basic regulation on child labor in the United States. Employers engaged in interstate commerce are not allowed to hire workers under 16 (or under 18 if the work is considered hazardous).

CHANGING ATTITUDES TOWARD PHYSICAL ABUSE

A little more than a half-century after passage of the Mann Act, the physical abuse of children finally began to receive some serious recognition as a pervasive social problem. In 1962 the *Journal of the American*

Medical Association first published articles on "battered-child syndrome." These articles showed that some families went beyond physical discipline—actually putting their children's lives in danger. As the problems of battered children became better known, pediatricians became more sensitive to signs of abuse in their patients.

Legal definitions of abuse and neglect, and laws requiring teachers or doctors to report abuse, have steadily broadened since passage of the 1974 Child Abuse Prevention and Treatment Act (CAPTA), which established a standard system for handling child abuse cases. Still, individual states determine reporting statutes and investigative procedures. Under CAPTA, formal complaints increased from 669,000 in 1976 to 2.5 million two decades later. This increase is not due to more children being abused; instead, it is an indication of greater public sensitivity to child abuse. Unfortunately, CAPTA has also resulted in courts being more crowded with civil and criminal cases, leading many to push for restricting the law to clear-cut cases of sexual abuse, physical injury, young children left unattended, and facilitated delinquency.

CHANGING ATTITUDES TOWARD SEXUAL OFFENDERS

By the early 1980s the general public was forced to acknowledge the depth and breadth of child abuse in our society. Clearly abuse of children permeates all economic classes and ethnic groups. Incest is much more frequent than was once believed, and the results of childhood sexual and physical abuse were found to be longer lasting and more profound than previously thought. With several well-publicized cases in the late 1980s and 1990s, interest in child abuse grew.

The 1994 case of Megan Kanka, a seven-year-old New Jersey girl who was raped and murdered by a man who had previously been convicted of sex-related crimes, led to the 1996 passage of a federal law, popularly known as "Megan's Law." The purpose of this law is to arm communities with enough information to protect their children. Now when a convicted sex offender is released from prison, his or her description and whereabouts are given to local law enforcement—and, in certain circumstances the court deems appropriate, to neighbors, parents, and local community organizations where children are supervised. In some cases when a sex offender is paroled or released from prison, the family of the molester's victim uses the Internet to notify the media and other communities that might be affected by his or her release.

Jesse Timmendequas (bottom) was sentenced to a pair of consecutive life sentences for the 1994 rape and murder of seven-year-old Megan Kanka (left). Before this brutal crime, Timmendequas had already served prison time for sex-related crimes. As a result of this case a 1996 federal law, dubbed "Megan's Law," was passed; under this law, local police and community officials are notified when a sex offender is released from prison and moves into their neighborhood.

Because of the possibilities for widespread communication, civil liberties groups and others have argued that Megan's Law violates the rights of the sex offender, who has already been punished for his or her actions. Opponents of the law claim that if the person's criminal past is exposed when he or she enters a new community, it infringes on that person's rights to privacy and freedom from prejudice, and it restricts his or her chances to make a new life in a new setting. Others feel that state and federal governments should not interfere with family problems—the things that "go on behind closed doors." However, although this debate continues to rage, Megan's Law has been widely embraced by many communities nationwide.

Although CAPTA and Megan's Law provide federal guidelines for dealing with child abuse, most legislation regarding this subject is determined by the individual states. For instance, statutes outlining how a child can offer testimony vary from state to state. Kentucky is one of several states that requires accuser and accused to appear in court together; however, many other states will attempt to spare an abused child the pain and embarrassment of reliving the abuse in a public courtroom by allowing him or her to testify on videotape.

Clearly, child abuse remains a controversial issue. As it is, the United States' legal and social services systems can barely handle current caseloads. In response, the federal government is allocating funds to the state courts to help expedite child-abuse and custody trials and to make the courts more sensitive to the victims.

Feelings of fear, shame, and guilt are common in children who have been abused, either physically, sexually, or emotionally.

3

HOW ARE VICTIMS AFFECTED?

The effects of abuse on a young child can have both immediate and far-ranging consequences. The following case study illustrates how child abuse can affect or retard a person's development through adolescence:

■   ■   ■

Jenny, a 17-year-old girl, had been sexually abused by her father, a successful businessman and prominent member of the community. Starting when she was five years old and ending around her 12th birthday, Jenny's "respectable" father molested her through vaginal fondling, mutual masturbation, and oral sex. Her mother apparently saw signs of the abuse but refused to acknowledge it and acted as if nothing had happened. Finally Jenny confronted her parents by barricading herself in her room and refusing to come out. Only then did her father promise to stop abusing her. But the emotional damage had been done and still needed to be worked out.

While in psychotherapy, Jenny divulged that she had attempted to seduce other children in the past. When she was seven, she engaged in sex play with the other girls in her bunk at summer camp. At age ten, she initiated sex play with a boy by pulling his pants down, all the while telling him to keep it a secret. As a teenager Jenny compulsively initiated sexual contact with boys but would never respond to a boy who approached her first.

■   ■   ■

Abused children like Jenny feel powerless at the hands of a parent or other authority figure who victimizes them. Later on, especially during adolescence, it's not unusual for such children to try to make up for all the years of feeling vulnerable by striving for dominance in their relationships with peers—as Jenny did at camp and with her boyfriends. After all, sexually and physically abused children can't gain control over the relationship with their abuser, so they naturally try to achieve it elsewhere.

Researchers have found that being physically abused during childhood or adolescence may lead the victim to be more withdrawn and have lower self-esteem than classmates.

Being stigmatized through beatings, scapegoating (when a parent blames the child for the parent's actions), or sexual abuse makes a child feel shame and guilt, and lowers his or her self-esteem. The victim's sense of reality about the abuse is warped, for he or she is taught by the abuser that the beatings or sexual encounters are normal. Particularly in cases of sexual abuse, the adult perpetrator may tell the child that their time together is "special," leaving the victim to wonder why this "special" time feels so bad. The child's sense that what he or she is doing is wrong may be exacerbated by the abuser's insistence on secrecy, which is usually ensured by threatening the child with greater harm. A parent may warn that he or she will be sent to prison if the child tells anyone. In other words, the child is not only used as an object but is also made to feel responsible for the entire family's happiness. In Jenny's case, she also had to cope with her mother's disbelief and lack of protection. Such a reaction by the so-called nonoffending parent is not unusual and only serves to reinforce an abused child's natural tendency to repress traumatic memories of the abuse.

When a parent, who is supposed to be loving and nurturing, sexually exploits or physically abuses a child, the victim inevitably feels betrayed and has difficulty trusting others. Victims frequently distrust their own perceptions, credibility, and memory; in extreme cases this leads the victim to "block out," or deny, the occurrences of abuse. Children who have been abused may develop defenses that involve separating themselves mentally and psychologically from the experience to help them endure the abuse. For instance, a girl may try to remove herself from a traumatic situation by seeming to be asleep and acting as if the abuse is not happening. If this response continues for a long period of time, it could lead to dissociative identity disorder later in life (this psychological problem will be explained later in the chapter).

Children who have been physically and/or sexually abused may also suffer other symptoms, some leading to psychological disorders. It's not unusual for an abused child to grow increasingly anxious, which can result in nightmares, difficulty sleeping, and symptoms of post-traumatic stress disorder. Feelings of depression can be so strong that they cause low self-esteem and self-destructive behavior; some children may even attempt suicide. Physical health problems stemming from severe emotional strain can also occur. Another defense mechanism involves consciously splitting the parent into "good" and "bad" images to help the victim reconcile his or her confused feelings. Some victims of physical and sexual abuse may also suffer from episodes of paranoia.

Those who interact with abused children, such as classmates and teachers, have noted certain behavior traits. Peers find abused children to be antisocial, mean, and disruptive. Teachers have noted that maltreated children have lower self-esteem, are less comfortable in social situations, and are more withdrawn than nonabused children.

POTENTIAL FOR VIOLENCE

Many studies have found that childhood abuse and neglect, childhood family problems, and psychiatric problems are common among offenders convicted of violent crimes. Such a cycle of violence suggests that there is a relationship between childhood abuse and later antisocial, criminal, or violent behavior, including the abuse of one's own children. Childhood abuse may also contribute to other problems in adulthood, such as substance abuse and self-injurious behavior. Patterns of abuse in a family from one generation to the next have been related to such variables as abusive child-rearing behavior, marital conflict, severe physical punishment, parental alcoholism, mental illness and criminality, and financial stress. The theory is that the more negative factors stacked

Violence begets violence: when a parent is physically abusive, his or her children often become abusive when they are older and have families of their own.

against a family, the more severe a family's problems, and therefore, the greater the likelihood for later violence.

A 1996 study of 89 young prison inmates between the ages of 16 and 22 found that 86.5 percent of violent offenders (such as murderers or rapists) and 78.4 percent of property offenders had been physically abused as children. Several other studies have found similar results. However, although abuse and rejection have been found to be strong predictors of later criminal activity, they are not inevitable causes. Mitigating factors—such as individual personality, interaction with caring adults, and community involvement—can produce a more positive future for victims of child abuse.

The following case study illustrates how a child who has been physically abused may in turn abuse others.

■   ■   ■

Juan, an 11-year-old boy, was referred to a child psychiatry clinic after he forced his three-year-old half-brother to drink lye. Juan had returned to live with his mother and her boyfriend one year before this incident, after having spent the previous seven years with his father and stepmother in Puerto Rico. During this period, he had repeatedly been subjected to severe physical abuse by his father; this consisted of beatings on the head and burns inflicted on his little body with a hot iron. Since returning to his mother, Juan had become hyperactive and aggressive at home and in school, and he exhibited extreme resentment toward his two half-brothers, whom he had just recently met. He had hit both boys frequently before the lye incident.

Juan also confided to his therapist that he enjoyed catching mice, placing them in boiling water, and smashing their heads with a hammer, after which he would flush them down the toilet. When asked to explain this cruel behavior, he pointed to the scars and ridges on his scalp and the burn marks on his shoulder, exclaiming, "This is what my father did to me."

■   ■   ■

Victims of physical abuse often conclude that violent behavior is not only normal but also puts the aggressor in a preferable position—one of power. Juan had been taught by his father that physical battering was the way to react to stressful situations; thus, Juan handled his feelings of envy and resentment toward his half-brothers by attacking the cause of those feelings: his siblings.

Children who suffer familial abuse are made to feel loathsome and deviant by their parents. They may become suicidal or self-destructive; this reflects their belief that their abusive parent wants them to disappear. One of the more destructive behaviors in physically abusive families is role reversal, in which the child is expected to gratify the needs of the parent. A child may be given the sole responsibility for such household duties as cooking, cleaning, or infant care, and if he or she fails to complete the chores adequately, the child may be beaten. Such high expectations and repeated beatings leave many physically abused children with severe ego problems and delayed mental and physical development. They may feel a desperate need to please other authority figures, such as teachers or therapists, as a carryover from their need to please their abusive parents. On the surface these children may appear to be quite independent for their age, but deep down they feel depressed and needy, longing for loving contact but fearing it at the same time.

SHAKEN BABY SYNDROME

Although child abuse is becoming a more recognized problem in the United States, there is another problem that receives less attention: shaken baby syndrome. Shaken baby syndrome is caused by vigorous shaking of an infant or young child by the arms, legs, chest, or shoulders. There are an estimated 50,000 cases in the United States each year.

A baby's brain and the blood vessels that connect the brain to the skull are fragile and undeveloped. Forcefully shaking an infant causes its tender brain to tear loose from the blood vessels and slam against the skull wall. This often results in bleeding within the brain or tears in the brain tissue. This can cause brain damage, leading to mental retardation, speech and learning problems, paralysis, seizures, and hearing loss. In 25 percent of these cases, the baby dies as a result of the abusive shaking.

A forensic pathologist shakes a doll to demonstrate how brain damage can occur in infants when they are violently shaken.

Even if the child does not die, there are serious long-term ramifications that stem from shaken baby syndrome. The child may require expensive medical care to repair the damage or may need lifelong care to treat associated disorders such as cerebral palsy. In some cases, institutionalization may be necessary.

More than 60 percent of victims of shaken baby syndrome are male, and male parents or guardians are involved in 65 to 90 percent of all shaken baby cases. The number one reason the situation occurs is the caretaker loses control because of the baby's inconsolable crying.

Parents who are afraid they will hurt their child out of anger or frustration should follow three simple steps: (1) put the child in a safe place and leave the room for a few minutes; (2) calm down by taking 10 deep breaths or sitting down and relaxing for a minute; and (3) then return to the child and deal with the problem.

EFFECTS OF SEXUAL ABUSE

Many victims of sexual abuse become severely depressed, and some believe their bodies have suffered permanent physical damage from the sexual activity. Such feelings extend to fears that they won't be able to marry, get pregnant, or have normal babies. Sexually abused children who sustain genital trauma or contract a sexually transmitted disease are especially fearful of such long-term damage.

A parent who passively allows child sexual abuse to occur, like Jenny's mother in the case study cited at the beginning of this chapter, can cause a child to develop a distorted sense of self and reality. If the passive parent blames the child for participating in sexual activity, the child will naturally feel a greater sense of shame and guilt. He or she has no one to turn to for protection and solace.

Like physical abuse, *incest* (sexual contact between people so closely related that they would be forbidden by law to marry) can lead to role confusion. For instance, in a family where the father is sexually abusing his daughter, she may be treated like a spouse or confidante by her father. And if the mother is not emotionally or psychologically supportive, the daughter may be made to feel responsible for her father's happiness. A sexually abused child is often given the additional responsibility of keeping the family intact. Despite taking on the adult role, however, the child still feels an infantile attachment to the parent. Unfortunately, what the abused child really needs is protection, nurturing, and a sense of security.

At home and school, sexually abused children also tend to have low self-esteem and are typically unable to control their sexual impulses. For very young children this may mean a sudden awareness of genitals and sexual acts and words, and attempts to get other children to perform sexual acts. Additional signs that may suggest sexual abuse include exceptional fear of a person or of certain places, a strange response from a child when asked if he or she has been touched by someone, and unreasonable fear of a physical exam. As they grow older, some molested children experience an inability to enjoy sexual activity.

HOW COMMON IS SEXUAL ABUSE?

Sexual abuse accounted for 11 percent of the more than one million cases of child abuse substantiated in 1995 by child protective services. Or, according to a telephone survey of parents conducted by the Gallup Poll that same year, approximately 19 of every 1,000 children in the United States suffered sexual abuse. Girls were sexually abused three times more often than boys. Although these numbers are already large, researchers suspect that there are many other cases of sexual molestation or abuse that are not reported because of the attached stigma.

Discussing overall numbers of sexual abuse tells only part of the story. The type and frequency of abuse, ranging from relatively mild episodes that involve no physical contact to severe and repeated sexual violation, will cause varying levels of trauma in victims. The type of sexual abuse that is likely to cause the greatest problems involves intercourse, and particularly repeated occurrences of that abuse. In one study of 1,019 teenagers, more than one in every 20 young women and approximately one in every 70 males had been exposed to sexual abuse involving attempted or completed intercourse before the age of 16. Given the probability of underreporting, it is likely that these statistics are low estimates.

Sexual abuse affects children of all ages and from all levels of society. But it appears that, at least among reported cases, the majority of victims are at least eight years old and come from lower-income families. Those at highest risk of sexual abuse are females, children with parents who have serious marital problems, those who are emotionally distant from their parents, individuals whose fathers are extremely overprotective, and children of alcoholic parents. Certain home environments may also increase a child's risk of being sexually abused; inadequate parental supervision and inadequate education about the risk of abuse are two such examples.

THE LONG-TERM EFFECTS OF ABUSE AND NEGLECT

As many as 20 percent of the victims of childhood sexual abuse develop serious long-term psychological disorders. Childhood sexual abuse has been linked to the development of *post-traumatic stress disorder, dissociative identity disorder, mood disorders* such as depression, *antisocial personality disorder*, and *anxiety disorder*. Additional psychiatric disorders that usually appear during adolescence, or sometimes later in adulthood, are substance abuse and eating disorders. Victims may use drugs and alcohol to blot out the painful memories associated with the assaults, and eating disorders are some victims' way of dealing with problems of self-image, body image, and sexual identity. In general, sexual abuse does not inevitably result in psychiatric disorders, but it appears to increase a person's risk of such conditions; in other words, the more severe the abuse, the more vulnerable a victim is to later psychological problems.

In addition, women who have been sexually abused as children have an increased risk of being victimized again later in life by strangers and

Children who have been sexually abused often suffer from depression and low self-esteem, and may exhibit signs of fear or anxiety if their abuser enters their presence.

A common defense mechanism for children who have been abused is to "disassociate," or mentally remove, themselves from the abuse. Disassociative identity disorder is a psychological disorder sometimes seen in victims of abuse. Persons with disassociative identity disorder disconnect their thoughts, memories, feelings, actions, or sense of identity from reality during periods of painful or traumatic abuse. This provides a temporary mental escape from the trauma.

partners. A number of studies have revealed a wide range—anywhere from 33 to 88 percent—of victims of childhood sexual abuse who have later experienced a rape; only 17 percent of women who had not been sexual abuse victims experienced a rape. Often such repeated victimization has to do with girls being conditioned at an early age to assume abuse is normal.

POST-TRAUMATIC STRESS DISORDER

Among the problems commonly associated with childhood physical and sexual abuse or neglect are symptoms of post-traumatic stress disorder (PTSD). A child who suffers from this condition may experience the following symptoms:

- Intrusive, distressing memories and dreams of the traumatic event
- A desire to avoid people, places, situations, or activities that would remind the abuse victim of the traumatic event
- Diminished interest in previously enjoyed activities, estrangement from other people, or an inability to feel

emotions involving intimacy and tenderness (this is called "psychic numbing" or "emotional anesthesia")
* Persistent feelings of anxiety, irritability, and anger

Children who are abused by a parent or caretaker may withdraw from others to avoid the threat of interpersonal relationships. Such a defense mechanism might work for the child in the short term, but over time he or she will become seriously depressed over the loss of close personal connections. Either way, the child suffers emotional and psychological damage. A large-scale study of 12- to 17-year-olds indicates that out of the 5.7 million adolescents in the United States today who have been victims of either serious sexual assault or serious physical assault, nearly two million have suffered from post-traumatic stress disorder and more than one million still suffer from it.

DISSOCIATIVE IDENTITY DISORDER

Technically, dissociation is a mental process that disconnects a person's thoughts, memories, feelings, actions, or sense of identity from present experiences. Most people experience mild dissociations, such as daydreaming or "getting lost" in a book or movie, both of which involve losing touch with conscious awareness of one's immediate surroundings. However, those who suffer from extreme chronic dissociation in response to a traumatic event or series of events may become seriously forgetful and endure periods of amnesia, blackouts, and a severe inability to function in daily activities.

The 1973 case of Sybil Isabel Dorsett, which was turned into a book and a major film, introduced the term "multiple personality disorder." As a result of both horrific child abuse by her psychotic mother and her father's failure to rescue her from the abuse, Sybil's personality "split" into multiple personalities. Each of her 16 distinct personalities, 2 of whom were male, embodied feelings and emotions with which the "real" Sybil could not cope. Sybil herself was deprived of all these emotions and was therefore a rather drab figure. She was also unaware of her split personality. In certain situations Sybil's various personalities would appear. While these personas were in control of her body, Sybil suffered blackouts and did not remember the episodes. It was only the intervention of a psychoanalyst that alerted Sybil to their existence.

Sybil's condition has since been renamed *dissociative identity disorder*. The American Psychiatric Association changed the name in response to the highly emotional controversy surrounding such a diagnosis. Critics contended that "multiple personality" was misleading, as it implied several separate individuals occupying one person's body. In fact, only one person inhabits each body, and although the alternate personality states may appear to be very different, they are all manifestations of the single person.

People who chronically dissociate often refer to the experience as "spacing out" or "trancing." Such a reaction provides a temporary mental escape from the fear and pain of the trauma, and in some cases a memory gap occurs surrounding the experience. When faced with overwhelmingly traumatic situations from which there is no physical escape, a child may resort to "going away" in his or her head to avoid both the immediate physical and emotional pain and the anxious anticipation of that pain. By this dissociative process, the thoughts, feelings, memories, and perceptions of the traumatic experience can be separated off psychologically, allowing the child to function as if the trauma had not occurred. Over time, however, this mental escape can nearly become a personality trait, invoked whenever the child feels threatened or anxious. Repeated dissociation can also result in a series of separate identities, or mental states, like those developed by Sybil. Dissociative disorders also can lead to depression, mood swings, and suicidal tendencies. Some sufferers have experienced insomnia, night terrors, and sleepwalking, as well as alcohol and drug abuse, auditory and visual hallucinations, and eating disorders.

MOOD DISORDER

As indicated earlier, feelings of depression are common among the victims of abuse. These feelings are often linked with low self-esteem. The symptoms of depression include lethargy, a sense of worthlessness, lack of concentration, suicidal thoughts, disrupted sleeping patterns, and guilt.

ANTISOCIAL PERSONALITY DISORDER

Another psychological disorder that is commonly associated with child abuse or neglect is antisocial personality disorder. This condition is characterized by a persistent pattern of disregard for others or violations of their rights. Antisocial personality disorder usually begins in childhood or adolescence and continues on into adulthood. People with this disorder may express contempt for others around them, lack empathy or any feelings for others, and have an inflated sense of their own worth or position, often expressed as superficial charm. They fre-

Panic disorder, characterized by overwhelming anxiety and persistent worry or feelings of terror, is a type of psychological problem that can occur in conjunction with abuse.

quently have difficulty coping with boredom and controlling their impulses, and may complain of tension or mood swings. Violence and abuse of people close to them are other common behaviors.

ANXIETY, OR PANIC, DISORDER

Panic disorders are characterized simply by overwhelming anxiety and persistent worry or feelings of terror. They may be brought on by specific situations (for example, an abuse victim may feel terrified if he or she is returned to the scene of the abuse), or they may happen at random times without any noticeable trigger. The most common symptom of these disorders is a "panic attack," during which the person may experience increased heart rate, sweating, chest pain, or difficulty breathing. The intensity and duration of the negative emotion or reaction is disproportionate to the seriousness of any triggering situation or event.

Most serious cases of physical abuse are caused by male parents, stepfathers, or boyfriends who are angry or under extreme stress and take out their frustration on the child in their care.

4

WHO ABUSES CHILDREN AND WHY?

The media regularly remind us of the grim reality that innocent children of all ages have suffered the emotional, physical, and psychological traumas of abuse—and that their abusers come from all walks of life. Parents or caretakers are often responsible for physical abuse and neglect; however, sexual violators seem to snake through all regions of a child's small world: religious leaders, school staff, baby-sitters, neighbors, relatives, peers, doctors, and others.

What sort of person would physically attack or severely neglect an innocent child to the point of putting the child's life in danger? Though no single profile fits every case, studies conducted over the last few decades have found that, on average, most abusive parents are in their mid-twenties, live near or below the poverty level, often have not finished high school, are depressed and unable to cope with stress, and have been the victims of violence themselves.

A long-held belief was that severe abuse and neglect are largely caused by teenage or young single parents living alone. This has been contradicted by recent scientific data. In fact, six studies undertaken since 1988 have found that although abusive parents may have married in their teens, the abuse typically didn't start until years later and most of these parents were not raising their children alone. Examining deaths caused by abuse, one study revealed that 60 percent of the children who were killed had been living with both biological parents. A 1993 Missouri study showed that married couples represented half of the perpetrators of abuse and neglect deaths. Professionals who deal with such families report that many parents involved in fatal abuse and neglect are substance abusers with histories of child or spousal abuse.

A 1993 study by the U.S. Department of Health and Human Services found that children whose parents abused alcohol were nearly four times more likely to be maltreated than were children in non-alcohol-abusing families. In terms of specific types of abuse, they were almost five times more likely to be

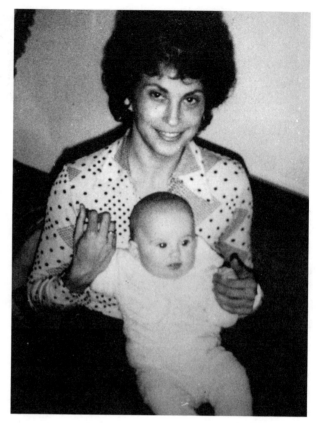

Hedda Nussbaum holds six-month-old Lisa Steinberg in a 1981 photo; little did she know that six years later she would be involved in one of the most notorious cases of child abuse. In the facing photo, a badly battered Nussbaum arrives at the police station with her husband Joel Steinberg on November 2, 1987. Steinberg had knocked Nussbaum unconscious, then beaten their adopted six-year-old daughter Lisa to death.

physically neglected and ten times more likely to be emotionally neglected. Other studies suggest that an estimated 50 to 80 percent of all substantiated child abuse cases involve some substance abuse by the child's parents.

VIOLENCE, STRESS, AND EXTREME ABUSE

Most serious physical abuse cases are caused by enraged or extremely stressed fathers and other male caretakers, including stepfathers and boyfriends. These men primarily assault infants and very small children by beating their heads and bodies, shaking them violently, intentionally suffocating them, immersing them in scalding water, or performing other brutal acts. And despite long-believed presumptions that mental illness is a leading factor in abuse and neglect, a 1992 study found that such impairment is a factor in only a small percentage of child maltreatment cases.

In 1987 the tragic death of Lisa Steinberg, who had been under the care of Joel Steinberg and Hedda Nussbaum, raised an important question: did Mr. Steinberg *intend* to beat Lisa to death? Lisa's short life began in 1981, when New York lawyer Joel Steinberg was hired to handle the newborn's adoption. Instead of placing her with an adoptive family, he and children's book author Hedda Nussbaum took custody of the girl, though they never legally adopted her. One night six years later, Joel first beat Hedda (apparently until she was unconscious) and then brutally beat Lisa into a coma from which she never recovered.

During Steinberg's trial, Hedda Nussbaum testified they had smoked crack cocaine in the hours before the beating and that Joel explained his attack as a reaction to Lisa's staring at him. (Charges against Nussbaum were dropped in exchange for her testimony against Steinberg; her lawyer argued that as a battered partner, she had been incapable of interceding on Lisa's behalf.) Joel Steinberg was convicted of first-degree manslaughter—not murder, because the court determined he had not intended to kill Lisa. He was sentenced to 25 years in prison.

Alcohol and illegal drug use are major contributors in cases of domestic violence, child abuse, and neglect of children. Studies have found that 40 percent of child abuse cases and 50 percent of neglect cases involve use of alcohol or drugs.

The judge recommended that Steinberg not be released before the end of his full sentence; as of January 1999, he has been denied parole twice since first becoming eligible in 1995.

Whether any parent or caretaker intends to hurt a child is difficult to judge, but it's a matter of great concern, especially in a court of law. It is difficult to believe that the broken bones, mental difficulties, and even death inflicted on so many children wouldn't make a reasonable person stop and question his or her actions. So why do some parents respond with extreme violence to natural events in a child's life, while others, suffering the same stresses, accept routine child-rearing challenges without resorting to violence? Researchers and practitioners continue to search for answers to this fundamental question. Whatever the reasons, getting to the aggressors before they strike could help to save many children from extraordinary pain and suffering.

ALCOHOL, DRUGS, AND CHILD ABUSE

In the United States, a large number of people have a problem with alcohol or drugs. In 1999, an estimated 20 million American adults abuse alcohol, and according to the U.S. Department of Health and Human Services the number of illicit drug users exceeds 12 million. There are 6.6 million children under age 18 living in homes where either one or both parents are alcoholics, and millions more living in households where a parent has a problem with illegal drugs.

NEGLECT AND MALTREATMENT

Recent research has indicated there is a link between substance abuse and child maltreatment. A 1996 study by the Children of Alcoholics Foundation found that 40 percent of the reported cases of child abuse, involving 480,000 children, involved the use of alcohol or other drugs. The percentage is even higher in cases of emotional abuse and neglect; alcohol and/or drug use has been linked to over half of these cases, and neglect is the major reason that children are removed from a home in which parents have alcohol or other drug problems.

Neglect may be the reason that children from homes with alcoholic or drug-abusing parents suffer from more mental and emotional problems than other children in the United States. These children often have more physical problems and illnesses as well, and are more likely to have behavioral problems and conduct disorder. The children lack guidance and positive role models at home, and frequently suffer from depression, anxiety, or low self-esteem. When they grow older, these children are more likely to have problems with alcohol and other drugs themselves.

FETAL ALCOHOL SYNDROME

The physical problems of children of alcoholics may have been caused by exposure to alcohol before birth. Women who drink alcohol while they are pregnant are more likely to have miscarriages, premature deliveries, or stillbirths than those women who abstain from drinking

PROFILE OF CHILD ABUSERS

I n an article in the June 22, 1984, issue of the *Journal of the American Medical Association*, Dr. Marilyn Heins of the University of Arizona College of Medicine grouped the factors that lead to child abuse into four categories:

1. A parent with the potential for abuse. Such parents are usually products of unhappy childhoods, often were themselves victims of abuse, are isolated, do not trust others, and have unrealistic expectations of children.

2. A child who usually exhibits some behavior that causes a strong correction reaction from the parent (for example, an infant that cries continuously or an older child who is disobedient or talks back).

3. A stressful situation or incident that serves as a trigger. This could be economic, such as loss of a job, or social, such as isolation from community support.

4. A culture in which corporal punishment is allowed or encouraged. "In one sense, all parents have the potential to abuse," Dr. Heins wrote. "But most of us keep our murderous capabilities in check because we have impulse control, inner resources, and support systems." The abuser, however, is lacking in one of these areas.

—Source: *Journal of the American Medical Association*

while they are pregnant. If the baby does survive, it may have serious health problems. Prenatal alcohol exposure is one of the leading causes of mental retardation. In 1973, the term *fetal alcohol syndrome* (FAS) was created to describe a pattern of abnormalities in children born to alcoholic mothers. Children with fetal alcohol syndrome may have had problems with the development of their central nervous system, resulting in mental retardation, undersized head and brain, or poor physical coordination; growth deficiencies in both height and weight before and after birth; facial abnormalities, such as short eye slits, droopy eyelids, thin upper lip, and mid-face and jaw deformities; and poorly formed organ systems, including heart, kidney, genital, bone, and joint. In addition, children with FAS can have problems with learning, attention, hyperactivity, memory and problem solving, impulsiveness, speech, and hearing. The children of drug addicts who continued to use drugs throughout their pregnancy are also likely to develop these types of problems.

Because these problems can add a financial burden to the family, the child may be singled out for undeserved abuse. Or, the substance abusing parent may put his or her child's life in danger by neglecting the health care required to keep the child alive and well.

DOMESTIC VIOLENCE AND CHILD ABUSE

Domestic violence is different from child abuse because it occurs when one member of a relationship, such as a parent, hits or abuses the other parent. It is defined by the National Committee to Prevent Child Abuse as "a pattern of assaultive and coercive behaviors, including physical, sexual, and psychological attacks, as well as economic coercion, that adults or adolescents use against their intimate partners." In 95 percent of cases, men are responsible for the assaults against their spouse, ex-spouse, or girlfriend.

There is a clear link between domestic violence and child abuse. Various studies (Jaffe et al., 1990; Straus and Gelles, 1990) estimate that physical or sexual abuse of children occurs in 30 to 50 percent of households where spouse-on-spouse abuse also occurs. The American Bar Association (ABA) reported in 1996 that "children in homes plagued by domestic violence may themselves be abused within those homes at a rate much higher than the national average for child abuse . . . overlap between households with both domestic violence and child abuse range from 40 to 60 percent." Because domestic violence is a pattern of behavior, not a one-time occurrence, it is likely that episodes of verbal or physical violence may become more severe. The abuser may eventually broaden his attacks to include the child or children in the family as well. Children may be hit or threatened by the abuser as a way of punishing or controlling the adult victim of domestic violence. They may be unintentionally injured by acts of violence that occur when they are present. And it is very likely that even if the children are not attacked directly, they will experience serious emotional damage as a result of living in a violent household.

Domestic violence, like child abuse, is not limited to any one economic level, race, region, or religious faith. Any family could have this problem—even the family of a young boy who one day would become the most important man in the United States, President William J. Clinton.

When he was growing up in Arkansas, Bill Clinton's stepfather Roger was an alcoholic and his mother, Virginia, also abused alcohol. When Roger Clinton was drunk, he often hit both his wife and children. Young Bill eventually became the protector of his younger brother Roger and of his mother. In Virginia's autobiography, *Leading With My Heart*, she recalled an incident when Bill was 14. Roger was beating her in their bedroom, and her husky son knocked the door down, grabbed his drunk stepfather, and ordered him, "Never . . . ever . . . touch my mother again."

Domestic violence and child abuse will occur in any environment that views women and children as less important than men, or overlooks incidents of domestic violence, rather than dealing directly and firmly with the perpetrators. "Shrouding the violence in secrecy allows this behavior to continue," says a 1996 fact sheet from the National Committee to Prevent Child Abuse. "Educating the public about the extent of the problem establishes a foundation that permits victims to come forward. Prevention efforts that reach parents before or soon after the birth of their baby, and provide intensive services on a moderately long-term basis can greatly reduce the incidence of child abuse as well as identify other problems such as domestic violence."

WHAT SETS OFF ABUSERS

Child abuse happens for many reasons, including immediate circumstances and the abuser's biological and psychological nature. Certain child-rearing situations are more likely than others to trigger battering: a baby's inconsolable crying, feeding difficulties, a toddler's resistance to toilet training, and highly exaggerated parental perceptions of disobedience. One study said that 80 percent of parents who abused children less than a year old gave excessive crying as the reason for the battering. Beatings are also triggered by stress unrelated to the child, such as a parent's loss of a job or a loved one, physical injury or illness, and legal difficulties. One of the more senseless cases of fatal abuse took place in Chicago in 1994, when the outcome of a televised sporting event prompted the father of five-month-old Roosevelt Bell to become so furious that he beat the boy to death.

Parental behavioral and personality factors and backgrounds that can lead to child abuse, violence, or incest include a history of being abused (emotionally, physically, or sexually), struggles with substance abuse, or chronic unemployment. In families where fathers are abusive, the mothers are often passive, dependent, and depressed, often with a history of abuse and victimization. In such situations, child abuse often begins with the battering of a spouse, then escalates to include the children.

A study examining the link between domestic violence and child abuse found that the probability of child abuse by a violent husband increases from 5 percent with one act of marital violence to a near-certainty with 50 or more acts of marital violence. In other words, each time a husband beats his wife, he is even more likely to beat their children. The case of Lisa Steinberg is a tragic example of such battering. Joel Steinberg had repeatedly beaten his partner, Hedda Nussbaum, prompting her to try to leave him five "and a half" times. The first time—the "half"—Steinberg came home to find her packing, beat her until she lay motionless on the floor, and then dumped her in an ice-cold bath. The final time, in November 1987, was after Steinberg reportedly went into such a rage that he knocked her unconscious just minutes before turning his anger on six-year-old Lisa. Like many women in abusive relationships, Nussbaum had never felt mentally or emotionally strong enough to leave. During Steinberg's trial, she maintained that the only reason she was finally able to leave was because she was carried out of the house.

■   ■   ■

Clearly, many factors can lead to child abuse. However, on the positive side, several factors also reduce the likelihood of abuse—including a parent's own history of good parenting and a secure, intimate relationship between the mother and father. In addition, children go through many phases of development—some more trying and stressful than others. During periods of relative harmony, parents are less likely to lash out at their children; they are also more likely to build up greater patience and tolerance over time. A sudden improvement in the family's financial conditions can act as a buffer as well. Generally, the more positive factors there are, the less likely it is that random stresses will lead to abuse. What is certain is that no one scenario leads unavoidably to child abuse, but many events along the way can shield a child from such trauma.

A former prep school teacher leaves court after his conviction for sexual assault in 1996. New Hampshire teacher David Cobb was convicted for trying to lure a 12-year-old boy to perform sexual acts on him, as well as for possessing and showing child pornography. In many cases, the sexual predator is a person who abuses his or her position of authority over a child.

5

SEXUAL ABUSERS AND THEIR VICTIMS

In chapter 1, sexual abuse was defined as any sexual behavior directed toward a child or adolescent under 18 by a person who has power over that youth. Some experts estimate that up to 90 percent of all sexual abuse cases involving children are committed by someone the child knows.

In cases involving children under age 11, males are more likely to be the sexual abusers than women. A large study of female adults who had been sexually abused as children (Bachmann et al., 1988) found that 53 percent were abused by biological fathers, nearly 15 percent by stepfathers, and 8.8 percent by uncles. Only 6.2 percent of the perpetrators were female. Strangers and other nonfamily members—such as neighbors, teachers, and acquaintances—comprised about 20 percent of the abusers in the study. A key distinction is that incidents involving family members are more likely to be severe and repeated. In fact, attacks by family members typically involve attempted or completed intercourse and occur over a longer period of time. Another large study of female adults who were sexually abused as children found that their abuse lasted an average of 7.6 years and began at age six. In contrast, the rates of intercourse or repeated incidents by acquaintances or strangers are far lower. As a result, sexual abuse within a family is likely to cause more serious damage to the child. These frequency and duration statistics reflect similar findings from many other studies of childhood sexual abuse.

JUVENILE OFFENDERS

Studies of incarcerated adult sexual offenders have shown that many sexual abusers had developed deviant sexual arousal patterns before they turned 18, in many cases when they were just entering adolescence. Historically, juveniles have not been held accountable for their sexual assaults. In fact, before 1985 reports of child sexual offenders were almost nonexistent. Their deviant behavior was considered to be exploratory, and the system didn't want to label

This psychologist is talking with young children about sexual abuse. Many times, the child will be encouraged to use dolls, like the one the therapist is holding, to indicate behavior that they were forced or urged to do by a sexual predator.

them for fear of stigmatizing them for life. As a result, truly accurate national estimates of children with sexual behavior problems have been difficult to determine.

In the last decade specialized programs have been developed to treat sexually abusive youths, leading to a better understanding of what makes them commit such crimes. The National Adolescent Perpetrator Network (NAPN) has provided data on more than 1,600 juveniles from 30 states who were referred to NAPN for specialized evaluation and/or treatment following a sexual offense. A common thread running through these youths' lives was a history of physical and sexual abuse, neglect, and the loss of a parental figure. Twenty-two percent of the youths who had been victims of sexual abuse reported that the person who sexually abused them was female. Most of their victims, in turn, had been females.

The FBI's 1990 Uniform Crime Reports indicated that 15 percent of the arrests for forcible rape were committed by youths younger than 18 years old, which breaks down to about 50 arrests per 100,000 adolescent males. Additional estimates suggest that adolescent males commit between 30 and 50 percent of child molestations. In Vermont in 1991, Social and Rehabilitation Services provided care to 135 children and adolescents who had engaged in abusive sexual acts, 51 (37.8 percent) of whom had done so before age 12. Of these 51 children, 47 were boys, and 36 were known victims of sexual abuse themselves. These 51 children were responsible for 13.2 percent of *all* child sexual abuse cases substantiated in Vermont in 1991.

MALE VICTIMS OF SEXUAL ABUSE

Until recently, boys were thought to represent an extremely small percentage of sexually abused children. One 1981 study put the total number of boys who had been sexually abused at 2.5 percent of the male population, while another estimated it to be 4.8 percent. A 1985 *Los Angeles Times* survey of the general population placed the number at 16 percent. Regardless of which is most accurate, reported incidents of sexual abuse against boys have risen steadily in the past decade.

Many believe that males who sexually abuse boys are homosexual; this is not necessarily true. In most cases, a man who molests boys is not expressing a homosexual orientation any more than one who molests girls is practicing heterosexual behavior. Although many child molesters do have gender and/or age preferences, of those who seek out boys, the vast majority are not homosexual. They are pedophiles, interested in sexually molesting almost any child.

Usually the use of adjectives like "homosexual" and "heterosexual" in child abuse cases refers to the abuser's gender in relation to that of the victim, not to the abuser's sexual orientation. Child molesters can be adult homosexuals, heterosexuals, or bisexuals. Their common link is that they prey sexually on children. The distinction between gender of victim and sexual orientation of abuser is important, because many child molesters have never developed the capacity for mature sexual relationships with other adults, either men or women. In general, adults who sexually abuse children fall somewhere along a continuum ranging from exclusive interest in children to interest in adults and occasionally children.

The victims of homosexual abuse may suffer added confusion about

British actor Roger Moore, best known for his role as James Bond in the 1970s and '80s, discusses his own experience with child sexual abuse. In August 1996 he told members of the World Congress Against Commercial Sexual Exploitation of Children that a pedophile had made sexual advances toward him when he was eight years old. The conference in Stockholm, Sweden, was aimed at stopping child prostitution and child pornography.

their own sexual orientation. For example, many boys who have been abused by males mistakenly believe that they themselves are homosexual or effeminate because something about them sexually attracts other men. This is not true. Yes, child molesters may be attracted to boys because of the child's lack of body hair and other adult sexual features; but the abuser's inability to develop and maintain a healthy adult sexual relationship is the cause—not the physical features of a sexually immature boy. Whether the abuse is perpetrated by men or women, a child's

RESPONDING TO CHILD SEXUAL ABUSE

I f a child tells an adult that he or she has been sexually abused, a supportive, caring response is the first step toward getting help for the child. The adult should encourage the child to talk freely, and should take what the child is saying seriously. The adult should listen carefully and be sure to understand what the child is saying. In child abuse cases, the adult offenders are always to blame because they are more mature and should know better. Abused children should never be blamed; they are victims.

A caring adult should reassure the child that he or she did the right thing in telling about the abuse, because the victim may feel guilty about telling if the abuser is a family member, friend of the parents, or a person in a position of authority in the community. The adult must indicate that the child is not to blame for the sexual abuse, because young children may feel that they caused or instigated the abuse, and promise to protect the child from further abuse.

Once there is suspicion of sexual abuse, it must be reported. If the abuse occurs within the family, it should be reported to the local Child Protection Agency. If the abuse is outside the family, the adult who is concerned about the situation should contact the local police or district attorney's office. The agency receiving the report will evaluate the situation and take steps to protect the child.

Parents concerned that abuse is taking place should take their child to their pediatrician, family physician, or a doctor who specializes in evaluating and treating sexual abuse. The doctor will examine the child to find if there are any physical problems related to the abuse, to gather information and evidence that support or dismiss the adults' suspicions, and to reassure the child that he or she is all right.

If child sexual abuse is found to have occurred, the victim should have a psychiatric evaluation to determine how the incident has affected him or her, and to determine if continuing psychiatric help is necessary to help the child deal with the trauma of sexual abuse. Other family members may also need counseling to understand and cope with the situation.

–Source: The American Academy of Child and Adolescent Psychiatry

Children who have been sexually abused may feel guilty if they tell someone else about what has happened. Feelings of depression are also common..

premature sexual experience can damage him or her in many ways, including confusing them about their sexual identity and orientation. But the experience does not mean that the victim will inevitably identify himself or herself as homosexual.

Although some women do sexually violate girls, these incidents appear to be uncommon. Most documented cases involve a female accomplice helping a male abuser to attract victims, or an adult woman seducing a young male.

YOUNG MALES SEXUALLY ABUSED
BY FEMALES

Although cases of females abusing males are considered to be unusual, they do occur. Recognition of such cases is limited to those males who have sought help in overcoming the stigma of psychological, social, and cultural presumptions about their sexual prowess. Even when a young man attempts to report unwanted sexual contact, his parents or other authority figures may fail to respond sensitively to the trauma. A number of widely held beliefs may be responsible for this aversion: that boys are rarely victims of sexual abuse; that perpetrators are always men; that young men usually enjoy sexual encounters with women; that sexual arousal in a boy indicates a willingness to participate in sexual activity. The following case illuminates how a young man can be affected by unwanted sexual encounters with a woman.

■   ■   ■

A 14-year-old boy named Billy was referred to a psychiatric clinic for evaluation and possible hospitalization for severe psychotic depression. He had become very despondent during the previous year and had become increasingly withdrawn, suffering crying spells and losing his appetite over the previous four months. He reported seeing objects moving about in his room at night and hearing voices calling his name in a deprecating way. He admitted having daily thoughts of suicide, at times quite compelling, although he had no specific plan. He was barely able to get out of bed. His family had no history of mental illness, neither did Billy have a history of substance abuse. Two other therapists had recommended hospitalization after a single visit each.

When his current therapist asked, "Is anyone treating you badly or have you ever been abused in any way?" Billy responded, "No." During the second session with the psychiatrist, however, Billy said he wanted to share some important information but that he felt very anxious. He finally revealed that for the past two years he had had sexual encounters with the mother of a boy for whom he baby-sat. These encounters included fondling, oral sex, and intercourse. Billy had never felt good about these incidents, and he had found them increasingly distasteful.

The present crisis was precipitated when he awoke while baby-sitting and found the mother lying on top of him, simulating intercourse. She persisted and Billy ejaculated. He felt angry and ashamed and ran from

When parents find out that a convicted child molester who has been released from prison is moving into their community, they often become concerned. Legislation such as "Megan's Law" makes this information available to local law enforcement officials, and parents have sometimes shared information over the Internet. These Oregon parents went a step further in August 1998; they offered to purchase the home that they are standing in front of, in order to prevent a man convicted of sex crimes from moving into the home, which had been owned by his mother.

the house. The woman followed him in her car and tried to entice him back to her home. He successfully returned to his own home but felt certain that he could not reveal the nature of this relationship to anyone. When asked about any previous similar abuse, Billy divulged that he had been fondled by a female baby-sitter when he was five years old.

When confronted by child protective services, the woman confessed, temporarily lost custody of her son, lost her job as a school teacher, and was enrolled under probation in a treatment program for sex offenders. Billy felt her punishment was appropriate, and his depression subsided almost immediately. However, a year later he still had difficulty handling the experience. He continued to have bouts of moderate depression and felt uncomfortable discussing his experience with anyone, including his therapist.

■　　　　■　　　　■

How frequently are females guilty of sexually abusing boys? Most researchers support the view that men make up the large majority of perpetrators against both boys and girls, but others speculate that female abusers are far more common than is usually believed. Of the sexually abused boys who telephoned a child abuse hotline in one year, 38 percent (some 400 children) had been abused by women: 18 percent by their natural mothers, 8 percent by sisters, 6 percent by stepmothers, and the rest by nonfamily members. The case reported here demonstrates why incidents of females sexually abusing boys are difficult but important to identify.

Premature or coerced sex—whether it is initiated by a peer, mother, older sister, baby-sitter, or other female in a position of power over a young man—causes confusion at best, and rage, depression, or other problems in worse circumstances. To be used as a sexual object by a more powerful person, male or female, is always abusive and often damaging.

Tragically, the members of our society who are the most defenseless—children—are too often the victims of abuse and neglect.

6

THE IMPACT ON SOCIETY

The overall impact of physical and sexual abuse of children has profound emotional and fiscal consequences for society as a whole. The debilitating effects of child abuse reach like tentacles across all areas of our lives, touching families and local communities, health care providers, the criminal justice system, welfare programs, and educational institutions. They are so pervasive that the U.S. Advisory Board on Child Abuse and Neglect has called the problem of child maltreatment in the United States "an epidemic."

At first glance, the financial strain this epidemic places on our society appears a minor, unimportant problem when compared to the suffering of innocent children, but the cost of abuse and neglect is a reality that cannot be ignored. For example, parents may want to overcome their abusive behavior and get treatment for their children but can't afford the bill for counseling. These families must either rely on state and federal assistance to help pay for the therapy or forgo treatment altogether. As a result, many children go untreated. This in turn leaves society at greater risk for the related negative effects of abuse.

How a person responds to being sexually, physically, or otherwise abused varies greatly, depending on the circumstances and personal characteristics of the victim. Abuse may be a one-time occurrence, and the victim might receive enough emotional support from others to overcome the trauma. However, experiencing abuse can lead to a wide range of problems throughout life, including criminal behavior. A 1992 study, which followed the developmental history of 1,575 children through early adulthood, revealed that those who had been abused or neglected as children were more likely to be arrested for a violent crime in adolescence and adulthood. Females were especially affected; although males generally showed higher rates of criminal behavior, young women who were abused or neglected in childhood were 77 percent more likely to be arrested than females who had not been abused. As adults, abused and neglected females were more likely to be arrested for property, drug, and misdemeanor offenses such as disorderly conduct, curfew violations, or prostitution, rather than for violent offenses.

Child abuse not only damages lives and adds rising rates of violence in this country, it also costs increasingly more money to treat and/or rehabilitate those involved. In 1993 the annual cost of responding to child sexual abuse in the state of Vermont was estimated conservatively at $42 million. The 1991 *Corrections Compendium*, a 10-year report of data from 49 state and federal penal systems, found that 85,647 sex offenders were incarcerated in 1990. And since the national average annual cost of housing one prison inmate is $24,000, the cost of incarcerating adult sex offenders in America in 1990 alone was $2.05 billion. Given the 48 percent increase in the number of incarcerated sex offenders in the two-year period of 1988–1990, and considering the current trend to impose more severe criminal sanctions in America, the cost of imprisoning adult sex offenders has grown considerably since that time.

CHILD DEATHS FROM ABUSE

The most serious cost is human life. According to the Population Reference Bureau, death rates among children four and under who die from homicide have hit a 40-year high. In other words, the murder rate of the very young by abuse is similar in scope to that of teenagers by street gunfire. Conservative estimates indicate that almost 2,000 infants and young children die from abuse or neglect by parents or caretakers each year; that's more than five children every day. The vast majority are under four, an age when they are most vulnerable to physical attacks and to dangers created by lack of supervision and severe neglect, and when they are isolated from teachers or others who might intervene to protect them.

Research at the Centers for Disease Control and Prevention (CDC) suggests that abuse and neglect kill 5.4 out of every 100,000 children age four and under. However, since many child deaths caused by abuse may be misclassified, a potentially more realistic estimate might be more than twice as high. In an extensive 1993 study to understand child abuse and neglect, the National Research Council (NRC) of the National Academy of Sciences noted that recent research suggests 84 percent of child abuse and neglect deaths have been systematically misidentified. Of the cases studied, 38 percent were listed as accidents, 15 percent as homicides with no indication that a parent or caretaker was the

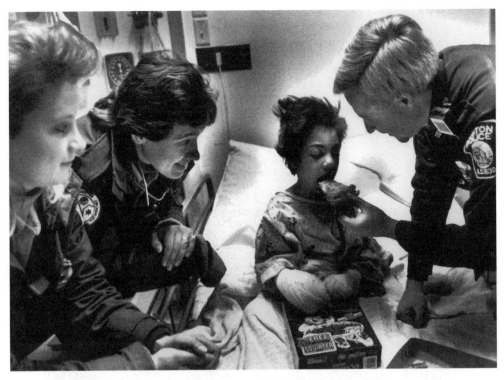

A police officer and two emergency medical technicians feed a piece of pizza to a four-year-old boy who was hospitalized after being abused and neglected. The child's mother burned his hands severely, then locked him alone in his room for a week.

perpetrator, 15 percent as sudden infant death syndrome (SIDS), 9 percent as natural, and 7 percent as "undetermined intentionality." Much of this misidentification is due to poor medical diagnoses, incomplete police and child protection investigations, inaccurate or incomplete crime reports, and flaws in the way the cause of death is recorded on death certificates. Such alarming levels of abuse deaths are particularly difficult to accept, given that death rates among infants and young children from all other major causes are steadily declining.

NEAR-FATAL ABUSE

Death from abuse and neglect is tragic enough, but each year the misery caused by near-fatal abuse leaves 18,000 children permanently disabled. Tens of thousands of victims struggle with lasting psychological trauma, not to mention the emotional impact on the thousands of

First Lady Hillary Rodham Clinton, a longtime advocate of women's and children's issues, receives a shirt from Jennifer Bush, an abuse victim, in August 1994. Jennifer had been hospitalized more than 200 times and accumulated more than $3 million in medical expenses; her mother was jailed for abuse.

siblings and family members. Many children with head injuries known to be caused by abusive caretakers are left with permanent brain damage and often require costly lifelong services. As adults, thousands of near-death survivors continue to bear the physical and psychological scars, causing many to continue the cycle of abuse themselves.

The National Center on Child Abuse and Neglect (NCCAN) esti-mates that 141,700 infants and children were seriously injured from abuse or neglect in 1990 alone. According to estimates, at least 10 times as many children survive severe abuse as die from it, and a staggering 9.5 to 28 percent of all disabled persons in the United States may have been made so by child abuse and neglect. However, no rigorous scientific findings exist for such disabilities. For example, of the 90,000 Americans left with brain damage from head injuries each year, the number caused by severe child abuse or neglect is unknown.

In addition to the terrible price these children pay, society spends an estimated average of $20,000 per year for services throughout the life of each child with an acquired disability. Clearly the millions now being spent to care for victims would be far better and more humanely spent developing services and strategies to prevent and reduce injuries. The National Research Council (NRC) pointed out in 1993 that in the long run "the future lost productivity of severely abused children is $658 million to $1.3 billion, if their impairments limit their potential earnings by only five to ten percent." Of course, money is not the only issue. More important is the deteriorated quality of life and loss of independence for the victims themselves.

INCREASING PUBLIC AWARENESS

Public concern over the crisis of child abuse is growing, in large part because of intense media coverage. Documentaries and media reports, such as Gannett News Service's 1990 Pulitzer Prize-winning exposé "Getting Away with Murder" and the *Chicago Tribune*'s 1994 Pulitzer finalist "Killing Our Children," have done much to awaken the public to the horror of child abuse and deaths.

Stirred up by the media, society has also gotten caught up in the controversy about adult recollection of childhood sexual abuse. When such cases initially emerged, we were shocked, feeling only sympathy for the victims and outrage toward the attackers. Eventually, however, news stories about recovered memories of sexual abuse began running opposing views about the veracity of such accounts. No longer was the focus of media attention on the alarmingly high incidence of child sexual abuse, thereby drawing attention to a long-hidden problem. Instead, between 1992 and 1994 approximately three-fourths of the articles about child sexual abuse focused on the issue of false accusations and false memories, questioning the character of victims and emphasizing the damage caused to families and wrongly accused individuals.

Currently, journalism organizations are making an effort to establish industry-wide standards that are more objective and sensitive to the rights of child abuse victims. As time goes on, the debate over false memories will likely die down; society has been confronted with too many cases of child abuse to deny that it occurs all too frequently.

As these children's signs say, there is no excuse for child abuse. They are part of a
1996 protest outside the U.S. Supreme Court that was organized during a hearing for a
woman accused of kidnapping and abusing a newborn baby.

TREATMENT AND PREVENTION

Children who have been abused can be treated, but first the abuse must be identified and reported. In both 1995 and 1996, child protective services agencies investigated an estimated two million reports alleging the maltreatment of almost three million children. In those years, according to the U.S. Department of Health and Human Services, between one-half and two-thirds of the reports came from professionals such as teachers, law enforcement or court officials, medical and mental health professionals, social service workers, and child care providers. About 19 percent of the reports came from relatives of the child or from the abused child.

Once a report of suspected child abuse is made, the case is checked into by the police or a social service agency. The child is typically examined by a doctor, who consults with the investigator and looks for signs of physical or sexual abuse. If the abuser is a family member, the local social services agency or child protection agency will usually handle it. When a child is abused by a nonfamily member, the matter is usually handled by the police.

What happens next depends on the circumstances, especially on the degree of risk to the child's safety. In many cases the abuser or the entire family may be required to attend a treatment program. Some offenders may even face criminal charges. If the child's safety is in question, he or she may be removed from the home.

STOPPING AND TREATING PHYSICAL ABUSE

Ideally, the best way to treat physical abuse and neglect is to prevent them from occurring. Of course, it's impossible to be in every home for every crisis, so child protective services agencies and hospitals rely on those who come in contact with children—teachers, doctors, relatives—to notify them about cases of suspected child abuse. Types of abuse can vary from supervisory neglect, in which the child is not being taken care of properly for extended periods of time, to severe physical battering that results in death. Relatively mild forms of abuse may simply require training the parents to better understand the vulnerability of such young lives. Groups like Parents Anonymous have emerged to help abusive parents. However, the more serious physical beating of a child may result in the child being placed in a treatment center or foster home while the parents undergo therapy to overcome, or at least manage, their violent tendencies.

In other cases children who have been abused are not discovered (and helped) until they, in turn, abuse. After repeatedly being beaten by their own parents, children may turn around and imitate such aggressive and violent behavior elsewhere. They may take it out on siblings or schoolmates, conduct that will likely land the abusive child in a psychiatric clinic for evaluation and treatment.

Chapter 3 introduced the case of Juan, the 11-year-old who had made his young brother drink lye. As a result of this incident, Juan started undergoing therapy, which revealed that he felt jealous of his half-brothers as new sibling rivals. Naturally, it also brought out his feelings about his father, who had beaten him. Apparently, Juan had identified with his father's aggressive nature, and in an attempt to build his own self-esteem he had taken his rage out on his half-brothers (and the mice that he admitted destroying). With the help of the therapist, Juan felt encouraged to verbalize the rage, helplessness, and fear he experienced during beatings, and he began to feel more secure in his new home. In turn, his desire to emulate such violent behavior diminished.

TREATING SEXUAL ABUSE

Over the last decade, hundreds of specialized sexual abuse treatment programs have been established. Of the hundreds of thousands of substantiated cases of sexual abuse, anywhere from one-half to three-quarters of the victims are likely to undergo some form of counseling or psychotherapy in treatment programs or with generalist clinicians.

The focus of treatment for sexual abuse varies according to how the victims have reacted to the trauma. Are they showing signs of post-traumatic stress disorder? Do they suffer anxiety and panic attacks? Have they tried to injure themselves physically? Is severe depression

Schools are an important place for children to learn about abuse. These middle school students are studying about sexual assault. Because teachers are in close contact with their students for a large portion of each day, they are often the first to notice signs of abuse in children.

bringing life to a standstill? In some cases victims who are already in treatment for something else, such as an eating disorder, find memories of sexual abuse begin to emerge. Each case is handled differently.

Depending on the severity of the symptoms, a therapist might recommend medication in addition to psychotherapy sessions. For those who reach periods of crisis, hospitalization is sometimes suggested as a temporary safe environment. Group therapy and support groups are considered helpful for breaking abused individuals out of depressive isolation. An emerging method of treatment is art therapy, in which individuals are encouraged to express their pain and anger through painting, drawing, writing, or other art forms. No less important are friends, family, work, and school, which can provide stability and support outside of therapy.

The case study of Jenny, also introduced in chapter 3, describes how she had been sexually abused by her father. Jenny was quite depressed during the initial phases of treatment and allowed her therapist to read her diary. Her writing was filled with references to her self-loathing and her thoughts of suicide. It also discussed her anger toward both parents. The therapist helped Jenny to gradually acknowledge and verbalize her anger. As her rage mounted, she recalled that she had refrained from getting angry in the past because the family had been devastated by the sudden death of one of her older brothers when she was 14 years old. She felt that she had no right to get angry, because her parents were depressed and grieving over their loss. Once she began to express her anger, she was able to confront her parents about their respective roles in the molestation and its cover-up. She also arranged for a family session to be held in the presence of the therapist, at which time, using the therapist as a witness and ally, she made a list of demands: that her parents acknowledge their wrongdoing, apologize to her, and seek help for their problems.

HOW EFFECTIVE IS TREATMENT?

Therapy helped both Juan and Jenny come to terms with their abuse and gave them the courage to handle the fallout from confronting their fears. Indeed, a review of the effectiveness of treatment for sexually abused children confirms that therapy aids recovery—although some believe that recovery occurs over the course of time or because of some other factor outside of therapy, like supportive friends and family. One key finding of the review was that such problems as aggressiveness and sexualized behavior are particularly resistant to change, and that some children require more time and attention to overcome them (Finkelhor and Berliner, 1995). Clearly, prevention and treatment programs should constantly improve, based on research and practice; for many victims, however, therapy is a much-needed life preserver in turbulent waters.

THE OPTION OF ADOPTION OR FOSTER CARE

In cases where an abused child's life appears to be in danger, social service agencies may transfer the child from the biological parents' home into a treatment residence or a foster home. If the abusive parent undergoes treatment and can prove he or she is prepared to be a good caretaker, the child can be reunited with the family. If not, the child may stay in a foster home and eventually be adopted. Unfortunately, through all of the separation, loss, attachment, and possible reunion, the child endures great emotional and psychological stress. Many abused children have difficulty trusting adults; they vent their frustration through violence, depression, or other maladaptive behavior.

To help alleviate some of the stress on children who may spend too much time simply waiting for the child welfare system to process their case, the Fast Track Adoption Law was passed in 1997. This new law allows caseworkers to place certain children in foster homes much more quickly by reducing some of the red tape. Previously, states were required to use "reasonable efforts" to return a child to his or her home before placing the child in foster care. Now, in cases where parents have subjected the child to serious abuse, abandonment, or torture—or if one of the child's parents has been convicted of killing another child—the youngster can be placed in a more nurturing home as soon as a foster family is found.

PREVENTING CHILD ABUSE

To stem the rising tide of child abuse throughout the United States, many organizations and government agencies are refocusing their energy on prevention activities. Health care providers, community organizations, social service agencies, and schools, in particular, are becoming increasingly involved in the well-being of children and families. The following sections describe how these organizations are providing prevention services to strengthen and support families.

HEALTH CARE PROVIDERS

Doctors, nurses, and any other health professionals who see children and families during well- and sick-child visits are in a unique position to contribute to the family's overall well-being. Many of these professionals employ techniques to curb the onset of child abuse. For instance, prenatal and early childhood care can improve the health of new mothers and young children; family-centered birthing and coaching classes can strengthen the early attachment between parents and their children; visits to new parents at home—called "home health visits"—can inform parents of support, education, and community groups. Support programs in particular can relieve the stress experienced by parents of special-needs children.

COMMUNITY ORGANIZATIONS

Local groups that offer a wide range of services for children and families—such as social and recreational opportunities—include Boys and Girls Clubs of America, scouting troops, and YMCA/YWCAs. Families with limited resources, and hence increased stress, can tap the services of community centers, food banks, emergency assistance programs, and shelters. Self-help and mutual aid groups provide nonjudgmental support and assistance to troubled families. Child and respite care programs can reduce the stress that employed parents experience, and provide positive modeling and contact for parents and children.

SOCIAL SERVICE AGENCIES

Increasingly, welfare agencies and professionals are expanding their focus to include programs that prevent family problems from escalating into violence. Parent education services can help parents develop adequate child-rearing knowledge and skills. Parent aide programs provide supportive, one-on-one mentors for parents. During times of exceptional stress or crisis, parents and children can benefit from crisis and emergency services. Treatment for abused children may prevent or at least reduce the odds of multigenerational family violence.

SCHOOLS

With increased public and professional attention being given to the

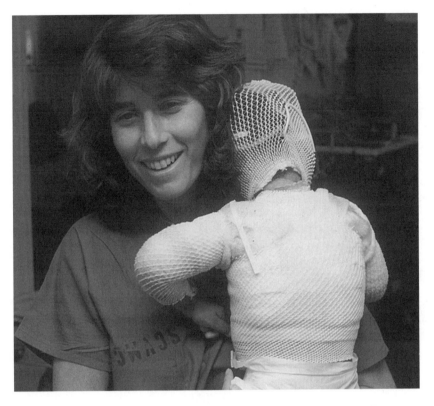

Doctors, nurses, and health care professionals are mandated to report cases of suspected abuse to the proper authorities—child welfare agencies or the local police. This nurse is holding a bandaged infant who was scalded with boiling water.

serious social problems affecting children and adolescents, many new abuse prevention efforts are focusing on school-based education. By learning about child abuse, what contributes to it, and how to deal with it, children gain valuable knowledge about what to do if they are in an abusive situation during childhood or adolescence. The introduction of school support programs for children with special needs has also helped to reduce the stress on families with a disabled child.

IF YOU ARE BEING ABUSED

If you are being abused, either physically, sexually, or through neglect, or you have a friend who you know or suspect is being abused, don't be afraid to talk to someone. Many times, an abused child feels that the abuse is his or her fault, or that he or she caused it by being

With continued education efforts, advocates hope that one day the terrible crimes of neglect and abuse against children will be eliminated.

"bad." This is not true: an adult or adolescent never has a right to beat or sexually abuse a child.

There are several people you can talk to about your problem. If the abuser is not a member of your family, then speak with your parents first. If you are being abused by a family member, tell a teacher or school counselor. If the physical abuse is so bad that you need medical help, don't cover up for the abuser—tell the doctor, nurse, or medical professional the truth about what has happened. In many states, teachers and medical professionals are required by law to report suspected abuse cases to the police and/or social service agencies.

If you can't find an adult who will listen to your story of abuse, you can try calling the National Child Abuse Hotline at 1-800-422-4453. The hotline is staffed by trained clinical psychologists who will discuss your problem with you. The counselor will then call a social worker in your area, who will meet you at school, away from the abuser, so that together you can plan the next step in ending the abuse. About one in four callers is an abused child; the hotline also takes calls from people who want to report suspected abuse and parents who are afraid they will hurt their child and want help.

■   ■   ■

The problem of child abuse and neglect of children is one that will not go away quickly or easily. Although attitudes toward punishment are changing, there are still too many children who are affected each year by the trauma of abuse. Sexual abuse of children also continues to be a concern for parents. Only through continued education, both of children and of their parents, can these problems be eliminated, allowing all children to live not in fear, but with hope for the future.

APPENDIX

FOR MORE INFORMATION

Many social service agencies and nonprofit organizations offer support and other services for victims of child abuse and parents under stress. Agencies can also be found in the telephone directory, usually with the state's listings, under Social Services, Protective Services, Social and Rehabilitative Services, or Children and Family Services. Many of the national groups also have state and local chapters.

Canadian Mental Health Association (CMHA)
970 Lawrence Avenue West
Suite 205
Toronto, Ontario M6A 3B6
(416) 789-7957

Childhelp USA/IOF Foresters National Child Abuse
Hotline: 1-800-4-A-CHILD
(800-422-4453)

Child Welfare League of America (CWLA)
440 First Street NW, Suite 310,
Washington, DC 20001-2085
(202) 638-2952

Effective Parenting Information for Children (EPIC) Program
Buffalo State College
1300 Elmwood Avenue
340 Cassety Hall,
Buffalo, NY 14222
(716) 886-6396

Father Flanagan's Boys' Home (Boys Town)
14100 Crawford Street
Boys Town, NE 68010
(402) 498-1301
Hotline: (800) 448-3000

Incest Resources, Inc.
Cambridge Women's Center
46 Pleasant Street.
Cambridge, MA 02139
(617) 354-8807

C. Henry Kempe National Center for Prevention and Treatment of Child Abuse and Neglect
1205 Oneida Street
Denver, CO 80220
(303) 321-3963

National Coalition Against Domestic Violence
P.O. Box 34103
Washington, DC 20043-4103
(202) 638-6388
TTY (202) 737-3033

The National Committee To Prevent Child Abuse (NCPCA)
332 South Michigan Avenue
Suite 1600
Chicago, IL 60604
1-800-CHILDREN (1-800-244-5373)
(312) 663-3520
Publications: (800) 55-NCPCA
(1-800-556-2722)

National Network for Youth
1319 F Street NW, Suite 401
Washington, DC 20004
(202) 783-7949

National Parents Anonymous
675 West Foothill Boulevard
Suite 220
Claremont, CA 91711
(800) 421-0353
(909) 621-6184

NAWA [an alternative to traditional education]
17351 Trinity Mountain Road
French Gulch, CA 96033
(800) 358-NAWA, (1-800-358-6292)

Prevention, Leadership, Education, and Assistance (PLEA) [for non-offending male survivors of abuse]
c/o Hank Estrada
Box 22, West Zia Road
Santa Fe, NM 87505
(505) 982-9184

Survivors of Violence
8031 Wadsworth Boulevard, #B4
Suite 104
Denver, CO 80021; (303) 940-6524
Denver metro area: (303) 201-3916

VOICES in Action, Inc.
P.O. Box 148309
Chicago, IL 60614

APPENDIX

QUESTIONS ABOUT SEXUAL ABUSE

The following questions are used to help victims of childhood sexual abuse recognize the particular problems that result from their abuse:

Self-Esteem: Do you often feel that you are not a worthwhile person? Do you feel bad, dirty, or ashamed of yourself? Do you have a hard time nurturing yourself? Do you feel that you have to be perfect?

Feelings: Do you have trouble knowing how you feel? Have you ever worried about going crazy? Is it hard for you to differentiate between various feelings? Do you experience a very narrow range of feelings? Are you afraid of your feelings? Do they seem out of control?

Your Body: Do you feel present in your body most of the time? Are there times when you feel as if you've left your body? Do you have a restricted range of feelings in your body? Do you find it difficult to be aware of what your body is telling you? Do you have a hard time loving and accepting your body? Do you have any physical illnesses that you think might be related to past sexual abuse? Have you ever intentionally hurt yourself or abused your body?

Intimacy: Do you find it difficult to trust others? Are you afraid of people? Do you feel alienated or lonely? Do you have trouble making a commitment? Do you panic when people get too close? Do you expect people to leave you? Have you ever been involved with someone who reminds you of your abuser or someone you know is not good for you?

—Source: McKinley Health Center's Counseling Center for Mental Health (University of Illinois Champaign/Urbana)

APPENDIX

BIBLIOGRAPHY

The American Academy of Child and Adolescent Psychiatry. "Facts for Families: Responding to Child Sexual Abuse" (pamphlet). Washington D.C.: The American Academy of Child and Adolescent Psychiatry, 1997.

Bachmann, Gloria, et al. "Childhood Sexual Abuse and the Consequences in Adult Women." *Obstetrics and Gynecology* (April 1988).

Bass, E., and L. Davis. *The Courage to Heal: A Guide for Women Survivors of Child Sexual Abuse*, 3rd edition. New York: HarperCollins, 1994

Children of Alcoholics Foundation, Inc. *Collaboration, Coordination, and Cooperation: Helping Children Affected by Parental Addiction and Family Violence.* New York: Children of Alcoholics Foundation, 1996.

Cicchetti, D., and S. L. Toth. "A Developmental Psychopathology Perspective on Child Abuse and Neglect." *Journal of the American Academy of Child and Adolescent Psychiatry* 34, no. 5 (May 1995).

Cruz, F. G., and L. Essen. *Adult Survivors of Childhood Emotional, Physical, and Sexual Abuse: Dynamics and Treatment.* Northvale, N.J.: Jason Aronson Publishers, 1994.

National Center on Child Abuse Prevention Research. *Current Trends in Child Abuse Reporting and Fatalities: The Results of the 1995 Annual Fifty State Survey.* Washington, D.C.: U.S. Government Printing Office, 1997.

Eagle, R.S. "Airplanes Crash, Spaceships Stay in Orbit." *Journal of Psychotherapy Practice and Research* 2, no. 4 (1993).

Fergusson, D. M., et al. "Childhood Sexual Abuse and Psychiatric Disorder in Young Adulthood: I. Prevalence of Sexual Abuse and Factors Associated with Sexual Abuse." *Journal of the American Academy of Child and Adolescent Psychiatry* 35, no. 10 (October 1996).

Fine, P. "Child Welfare Research Review." *Journal of the American Academy of Child and Adolescent Psychiatry* 34, no. 8 (August 1995).

Finkelhor, D. and L. Berliner. "Research on the Treatment of Sexually Abused Children: A Review and Recommendations." *Journal of the*

American Academy of Child and Adolescent Psychiatry 34, no. 11 (November 1995).

Flisher, A. J., et al. "Psychosocial Characteristics of Physically Abused Children and Adolescents." *Journal of the American Academy of Child and Adolescent Psychiatry* 36, no. 1 (January 1997).

Green, A. H. "Victims of Child Abuse." *Review of Psychiatry* 13, no. 4 (1994).

Haapasalo, J. and T. Hämäläinen. "Childhood Family Problems and Current Psychiatric Problems among Young Violent and Property Offenders." *Journal of the American Academy of Child and Adolescent Psychiatry* 35, no. 10 (October 1996).

Heins, Marilyn. "The 'Battered Child' Revisited." *Journal of the American Medical Association* 251 (June 1984).

Jaffe, P., D. Wolfe, and S. Wilson. *Children of Battered Women.* Newbury Park, CA: Sage Publications, 1990.

Janeway, Elizabeth. "Incest: A Rational Look at the Oldest Taboo." *Ms.* (November 1981).

Kilpatrick, D., and B. Saunders. *The Prevalence and Consequences of Child Victimization: Summary of a Research Study.* Washington, D.C.: U.S. Department of Justice, 1997.

Kinard, E. M. "Mother and Teacher Assessments of Behavior Problems in Abused Children." *Journal of the American Academy of Child and Adolescent Psychiatry* 34, no. 8 (August 1995).

Marmer, S. S. "Theoretical Foundations." In *American Psychiatric Press Textbook of Psychiatry*, 2nd ed., vol. 1. Washington, D.C.: American Psychiatric Press, 1994.

Peluso, E. and N. Putnam. "Case Study: Sexual Abuse of Boys by Females." *Journal of the American Academy of Child and Adolescent Psychiatry* 35, no. 1 (January 1996).

Pithers, W. D., et al. "Children With Sexual Behavior Problems, Adolescent Sexual Abusers, and Adult Sex Offenders: Assessment and Treatment." *Review of Psychiatry* 14, sec. 5. Washington, D.C.: American Psychiatric Press, 1995.

Putnam, F. W. "Posttraumatic Stress Disorder in Children and Adolescents." *Review of Psychiatry* 15, sec. 4. Washington, D.C.: American Psychiatric Press, 1996.

Roesler, T., and T. W. Wind. "Telling the Secret: Adult Women Describe Their Disclosures of Incest." *Journal of Interpersonal Violence* 9, no. 3 (1994).

Ross, S. *Risk of Physical Abuse to Children of Spouse-Abusing Parents.* Durham, NH: Family Research Laboratory, 1994.

Ryan, G., et al. "Trends in a National Sample of Sexually Abusive Youths." *Journal of the American Academy of Child and Adolescent Psychiatry* 35, no. 1 (January 1996).

Sedlak, A., and D. Broadhurst. *Executive Summary of the Third National Incidence Study of Child Abuse and Neglect.* Washington, D.C.: National Center on Child Abuse and Neglect, U.S. Dept. of Health and Human Services, 1996.

Spiegel, D. "Dissociative Disorders." In *American Psychiatric Press Textbook of Psychiatry*, 2nd ed., vol. 3. Washington, D.C.: American Psychiatric Press, 1994.

Stewart, D. E., and G. E. Robinson. "Violence Against Women." *Review of Psychiatry* 14. Washington, D.C.: American Psychiatric Press, 1995.

Straus, M. A., and R. Gelles. *Physical Violence in American Families.* New Brunswick, N.J.: Transaction Press, 1990.

Summit, Richard K. "The Centrality of Victimization: Regaining the Focal Point of Recovery for Survivors of Child Sexual Abuse." *Psychiatric Clinics of North America* 12, no. 2 (June 1989).

Tueth, M.J. "Psychopharmacological Treatment." In *The American Psychiatric Press Textbook of Psychopharmacology.* Washington, D.C.: American Psychiatric Press, 1995.

U.S. Department of Health and Human Services. *Child Maltreatment 1996: Reports from the States to the National Child Abuse and Neglect Data System.* Washington, D.C.: U.S. Government Printing Office, 1998.

U.S. Department of Health and Human Services. *The Third National Incidence Study of Child Abuse and Neglect.* Washington, D.C.: U.S. Government Printing Office, 1996.

U.S. Department of Health and Human Services, National Center on Child Abuse and Neglect. *A Report on Child Maltreatment in Alcohol-Abusing Families.* Washington, D.C.: U.S. Government Printing Office, 1993.

Williams, L. M., and V. M. Banyard. "Perspectives on Adult Memories of Childhood Sexual Abuse: A Research Review." *Review of Psychiatry* 16. Washington, D.C.: American Psychiatric Press, 1996.

APPENDIX

FURTHER READING

Baker, Robert A. *Child Sexual Abuse and False Memory Syndrome*. Amherst, N.Y.: Prometheus Books, 1998.

Carl, Angela. *Child Abuse: What You Can Do About It*. Joplin, MO: College Press Publishing, 1993.

Check, William A. *Child Abuse*. New York: Chelsea House, 1989.

Crewdson, John. *By Silence Betrayed: Sexual Abuse of Children in America*. Boston: Little, Brown, 1988.

Delaplain, Laura. *Cutting a New Path: Helping Survivors of Childhood Domestic Trauma*. New York: United Church Press, 1997.

Dziech, Billie Wright, and Charles B. Schudson. *On Trial: America's Courts and Their Treatment of Sexually Abused Children*. Boston: Beacon Press, 1989.

Freyd, Jennifer J. *Betrayal Trauma: The Logic of Forgetting Childhood Abuse*. Cambridge, Mass.: Harvard University Press, 1996.

Golbert, Neil, ed. *Combatting Child Abuse: International Perspectives and Trends*. New York: Oxford University Press, 1997.

Goldentver, Debra. *Child Abuse*. Austin, Texas: Raintree/Steck Vaughn, 1998.

Gruban-Black, Stephen D. *Broken Boys/Mending Men: Recovery from Childhood Sexual Abuse*. New York: Ivy Books, 1997.

Heineman, Toni Vaughn, Toni V. Heineman, and Alicia F Lieberman. *The Abused Child: Psychodynamic Understanding and Treatment*. New York: The Guilford Press, 1998.

Helfer, Mary Edna, Ruth S. Kempe, and Richard D. Krugman, eds. *The Battered Child*. 5th edition. Chicago: University of Chicago Press, 1997.

Iwaniec, Dorota. *The Emotionally Abused and Neglected Child: Identification, Assessment, and Intervention*. Englewood, N.J.: John Wiley & Sons, 1995.

Jaffe, P., D. Wolfe, and S. Wilson. *Children of Battered Women*. Newbury Park, Calif.: Sage Publications, 1990.

Kendig, Bobbi, and Clara Lowry. *Cedar House: A Model Child Abuse Treatment Program.* Binghamton, N.Y.: The Haworth Press, 1998.

Markham, Ursula. *Childhood Trauma: Your Questions Answered.* New York: Element Books, 1998.

Melton, G. B., and F. B. Barry, eds. *Protecting Children from Abuse and Neglect.* New York: Guilford Press, 1994.

Sanders, Pete, Steve Myers, and Mike Lacey. *What Do You Know About Child Abuse?* Providence, R.I.: Copper Beech Books, 1996.

Straus, M. A., and R. Gelles. *Physical Violence in American Families.* New Brunswick, N.J.: Transaction Press, 1990.

Trager, James. *The People's Chronology.* New York: Henry Holt and Company, 1994.

Abandonment: To desert someone or something; the practice of leaving a child alone for a period of time.

Antisocial personality disorder: A psychological disorder characterized by a persistent pattern of disregard for others or violations of their rights. Antisocial personality disorder usually begins in childhood or adolescence and continues into adulthood.

Anxiety disorder: A group of psychological disorders, such as panic disorder, characterized by extreme stress, nervousness, or anxiety in situations that should not cause such severe reactions. Anxiety disorders may occur if an abused child is returned to the scene of his or her abuse, or placed in a situation similar to the one in which the abuse occurred.

Child abuse: Physical or emotional maltreatment of a child or adolescent. Child abuse consists of four categories: neglect, physical abuse, sexual abuse, and emotional abuse.

Dissociative identity disorder: A psychological disorder sometimes seen in victims of abuse. Persons with dissociative identity disorder disconnect their thoughts, memories, feelings, actions, or sense of identity from reality during periods of painful or traumatic abuse. This provides a temporary mental escape from the trauma. In the most severe cases, such as the 1973 case of Sybil Isabel Dorsett, the victim may develop multiple personalities.

Emotional abuse: Abuse of a child in the form of verbal insults, belittling, or blaming the child for problems that are beyond his or her control. Emotional abuse, sometimes called "psychological abuse," may cause the child to develop severe behavioral, emotional, or mental disorders.

Fetal alcohol syndrome: A collection of problems that affect an unborn child, associated with the mother's consumption of alcohol during pregnancy; these include growth deficiencies and underdevelopment of the central nervous system and other body organs.

Incest: Sexual contact between persons so closely related that they are forbidden by law to marry.

Mood disorders: A group of psychological disorders, including depression and manic depression, characterized by extreme mood swings that impair a person's ability to function normally in society. In severe cases mood disorders can drive a person to attempt suicide. These disorders often occur in children who are neglected or physically, sexually, or emotionally abused.

Neglect: When a parent or guardian chooses not to meet the basic physical, emotional, or educational needs of a child. Physical neglect occurs when the child is abandoned or forced out of the home, or when the parents refuse to take a sick child to the hospital. If the child is repeatedly deprived of affection, this qualifies as emotional neglect. Educational neglect involves failing to enroll a child in school or ignoring a child's special education needs.

Physical abuse: Infliction of injury on a child or adolescent by an adult, usually a parent or guardian. Common forms of abuse include hitting, kicking, biting, burning, or violently shaking the child.

Pornography: Films, pictures, or literature intended to arouse sexual excitement.

Post-traumatic stress disorder: A chronic mental disorder that appears in victims of abuse. Post-traumatic stress disorder occurs after a traumatic or stressful event; its symptoms include distressing memories or dreams of the event that the victim attempts to suppress; a desire to avoid people, places, situations, or activities that would remind the victim of the abuse; diminished interest in previously enjoyed activities; and persistent feelings of anxiety, irritability, and anger.

Sexual abuse: Sexual exploitation of a child by an adult or an older person in a position of authority. Sexual abuse may involve physical sexual contact, exhibitionism, showing a child pornography, or involving the child in making pornographic materials.

Shaken baby syndrome: Bleeding and damage to the brain of an infant caused by forceful and repeated shaking of the body. This can lead to mental retardation, permanent brain damage, or death.

APPENDIX

INDEX

APPENDIX

PICTURE CREDITS

page

Senior Consulting Editor Carol C. Nadelson, M.D., is president and chief executive officer of the American Psychiatric Press, Inc., staff physician at Cambridge Hospital, and Clinical Professor of Psychiatry at Harvard Medical School. In addition to her work with the American Psychiatric Association, which she served as vice president in 1981–83 and president in 1985–86, Dr. Nadelson has been actively involved in other major psychiatric organizations, including the Group for the Advancement of Psychiatry, the American College of Psychiatrists, the Association for Academic Psychiatry, the American Association of Directors of Psychiatric Residency Training Programs, the American Psychosomatic Society, and the American College of Mental Health Administrators. In addition, she has been a consultant to the Psychiatric Education Branch of the National Institute of Mental Health and has served on the editorial boards of several journals. Doctor Nadelson has received many awards, including the Gold Medal Award for significant and ongoing contributions in the field of psychiatry, the Elizabeth Blackwell Award for contributions to the causes of women in medicine, and the Distinguished Service Award from the American College of Psychiatrists for outstanding achievements and leadership in the field of psychiatry.

Consulting Editor Claire E. Reinburg, M.A., is editorial director of the American Psychiatric Press, Inc., which publishes about 60 new books and six journals a year. She is a graduate of Georgetown University in Washington, D.C., where she earned bachelor of arts and master of arts degrees in English. She is a member of the Council of Biology Editors, the Women's National Book Association, the Society for Scholarly Publishing, and Washington Book Publishers.

As director of Write Stuff Editorial Service in New York City, **Elizabeth Russell Connelly** has written and edited for medical and business journals, trade magazines, high-tech firms, and various book publishers. She earned an MBA from New York University's Stern School in 1993 and a certificate in language studies from Freiburg Universitaet (Switzerland) in 1985. Her published work includes a global studies book for young adults; more than 14 Access travel guides covering North America, the Caribbean, and Europe; and several volumes in Chelsea House Publishers' ENCYCLOPEDIA OF PSYCHOLOGICAL DISORDERS.